THE MACMILLAN SPELLING SERIES 6

Revised Edition

General Editor:

George E. Flower
Dean, Faculty of Education
McGill University, Montreal

Authors:

Robert F. Bornhold
K. H. D. Hall
Robert J. Ireland
Gordon F. Mann
Sybil Shack

Designed by Glyphics
Division of
Kerrigan O'Grady Limited

Illustrated by Heather Collins

©1961, Revised Edition 1978, The
Macmillan Company of Canada Limited,
70 Bond Street, Toronto M5B 1X3
Affiliated with Maclean-Hunter
Learning Materials Company.

Canadian Cataloguing in Publication Data

Ireland, Robert J., date
  The Macmillan spelling series, 6

ISBN 0-7705-1551-7

1. Spellers. I. Title.

PE1145.2.I76 1977   428'.1   C77-001615-4

Printed in Canada

THE MACMILLAN SPELLING SERIES 6

Revised Edition

Robert J. Ireland

Macmillan of Canada

To the Teacher

The aim of instruction in spelling is to enable each pupil to spell correctly each word he or she writes. The seven books of The Macmillan Spelling Series are therefore designed:

- To teach pupils automatic mastery of the words that they need for writing; to develop, that is, the ability to spell correctly all written work in and out of school, not just words in lists in spelling periods.

- To develop self-dependence in spelling: the ability to locate correct spellings and check the accuracy of spelling.

- To develop pride and interest in spelling correctly.

- To enable the teacher to provide for individual differences in spelling ability.

In order to achieve these aims The Macmillan Spelling Series includes materials:

- To help pupils acquire an efficient method of studying and mastering the spelling of words.

- To make the study of spelling interesting and productive by giving pupils the opportunity to do a variety of exercises that direct attention to the meaning, use, and structure of the words in the spelling lists.

- To provide remedial practice.

- To provide enrichment activities.

This book consists of forty units, including seven review units. Four hundred and thirty-seven words are listed, of the total list for the series of 2934. The 2608 words in the series' basic list are those most frequently written by children and provide for about ninety-five per cent of the average pupil's needs. In addition to the basic list, the series contains 326 extra words, of which forty-nine are included here.

The words in this book are grouped in such a way as to aid learning and to allow for the development of spelling power well beyond the basic list through word analysis, word building, comprehension, and use. Since pupils vary widely in spelling aptitude and achievement, extra words have been included from time to time, as well as special activities for good spellers and for less able ones in each review unit. Where extra words are listed in a unit, they appear in a separate colour block. Repeated attention is given to the 282 words studied so far in the series of the approximately 330 words that account for the great majority of all spelling errors.

A Teacher's Handbook for each book in the series is available. Included in the handbook, unit by unit, are guides for teaching and re-teaching difficult words, answers to exercises, background material for the teacher, further suggestions for relating spelling to other parts of the language arts program, and extra exercises for both good and less able spellers. The extra exercises are also available separately, in reproducible form.

To the Pupil

How To Study a Word

Follow these five
steps in learning
to spell a word:

5. Practise
4. Check
3. Write
2. Think
1. Look

1. **Look** at the word.
   - Look at it from left to right.
   - Look at the letters from left to right.
   - Say the letters to yourself.
   - Say the word carefully.

2. **Think** about the word.
   - Close your eyes. Try to remember what the word looks like.
   - Spell the word to yourself.
   - Check this first attempt.

3. **Write** the word.

4. **Check** how you spelled it.
   - Did you get it right?
   - If not, look for the part of the word that was hard for you. Write the word correctly.

5. **Practise** spelling the word.
   - Start again at step 1, until you are sure that you can spell the word correctly.
   - Write a sentence using the word. Check the spelling in the sentence.

1 Play Ball!

pitcher	signal	major	practice
league	board	lose	practises
strikes	steal	losing	championship
risk	stole	racket	

1. Use words from the list to answer these questions about the picture.
   (a) Who is throwing the ball?
   (b) Where do you see the score?
   (c) How many strikes has the umpire called?
   (d) What is the runner trying to do?

2. (a) **Practice** is a noun and **practises** is a verb. Write both words and circle the letter in each one that shows the difference between the noun and the verb.
   (b) Nouns are words that may be made plural. Write the plural form of **practice.**
   (c) Many verbs can have **ing** added to the base. Write the **ing** form of **practise.**

3. Home Run!
   Draw a small baseball diamond like the one below. You get to first base by writing a word from the list. That's easy. To get "home", you must write three other words that are formed from the one you just wrote. You may add prefixes or suffixes (including **ed** or **ing**), or you may change the form of the word. For example, **steal-stole** are different forms of the same word. How many runs can you score?

4. (a) Write the word in the list that is formed from **sign.**
   (b) What is the difference in the pronunciation of **g** in **sign** and in the word in the list?
   (c) Write **championship.** What is the base word?
   (d) Which word in the list has three silent vowels?

5. (a) Which word in the list could mean the noise that the crowd makes at a baseball game?
   (b) The same word could mean something used in another sport. Write an answer to this question using the same word you wrote in (a): What do you use to hit a tennis ball?

6. (a) Which word could mean take a chance?
   (b) What are two ways that you might take a chance when you are playing baseball? Use the word you wrote in (a) in answering.

7. Tell what the words in heavy type mean in the sentences below.
   We saw a **major league** baseball game.
   He is a **major** in the armed forces.

8. Tell two meanings of the sentence below.
   The pitcher fell off the table.

9. It is the last inning of the championship game. Your team is behind by one run. There are two people on base. You come to bat. How do you feel? What are you thinking about? Use these ideas and some of your own to write a story about a baseball game.

The Many Voices of G

ledge			
synagogue			
hinge			

beginning	knowledge	dodge	general
voyage	dining	refrigerator	sausage
imagine	eighth	interesting	

The letter **g** has many voices. It sometimes sounds like a **j**. It is often sounded with **n** to give the sound at the end of **ring**. Sometimes it has its own sound, as in **league** in Unit 1. Sometimes the **g** is silent.

1. (a) Write the words in the list in which **g** sounds like **j**.
    (b) Circle the letter that comes after the **g** in the words you just wrote.
    (c) In which word in the list is the **g** silent?

2. (a) Which words in the list end in **ing**? Beside each, write the base form of the word.
   (b) What is the base form of **knowledge, eighth, dining**?

3. (a) Write **refrigerator**. Underline the prefix in that word.
   (b) Make new words from **imagine**. First write **imagine**. Then drop the **e** and add **ary** and then **ation**.

4. (a) Write **voyage** and four other words you know that end in **age**. Hint: Two words that end that way could both mean suitcases.
   (b) Write the number of each of these places. After each number write **voyage** if you would use that word to describe a trip to that place.
      (i) the moon
      (ii) the corner store
      (iii) China

5. Which words in the list could have these meanings?
   - an army officer
   - to get out of the way
   - learning
   - starting
   - pretend

6. What is the difference between a sausage and a wiener?

7. The root of **refrigerator** is a Latin word, **frigus**, meaning cold. Write another word from the same root that we could use in talking about a very cold climate.

8. Just what you dreamed about! An ocean voyage! But wait a minute. The ship looks very old and small. You can hardly fit all your things into your cabin. When the trip starts the ship rolls back and forth. What problems does this cause? What other discoveries do you make about the ship? Write a story telling about your ocean voyage that was not what you expected it to be.

3 Cooking and Baking

flour	slice	knife	recipe	
kitchen	sour	mix	saucer	syrup
oven	spoon	jelly	crust	
soup	toast	stir	yeast	

1. (a) Arrange all the one-syllable words in the list in alphabetical order.
   (b) Which two words in the list rhyme?
   (c) Another word in the list has the same vowel pair as the words in (b), but a different vowel sound. Write the word and tell what sound the vowels make.
   (d) Write **spoon** and **soup**. Circle the vowels in each word and tell the sound each makes.
   (e) Write **saucer**, **toast**, and **yeast**. Circle the vowel pairs in these words and tell the sound each makes.

2. (a) **Jelly** and **gelatin** come from the same root and are similar in meaning. Which do you think is the older word? Tell why you think so.
   (b) What part of a stove is used for baking?
   (c) Write **crust**. Make a new word by adding one letter to **crust**. Use your new word in a sentence.

3. (a) Which words begin with the sound /k/?
   (b) Which word begins with a silent **k**? Write three other words you know that begin the same way.
   (c) In which words does the letter **c** have the /s/ sound?

4. Write **spoon**. Make compound words by adding **ful, tea, table**.

5. Write
   (a) **mix**; make a new word by adding **ture**.
   (b) the plural of **mix, jelly,** and **knife**.
   (c) **toast, slice, stir**; to each add **ing**; what changes must you make in some of the base words?

6. Kitchen Puzzle
   Write **kitchen** on your page as it is written below. Be sure to have the correct number of spaces above and below it. Circle the spaces that are circled below. Use the clues to fill in the spaces.

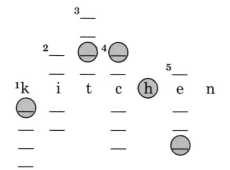

Clues
1. sharp pointed instrument
2. thin strip
3. outer part of bread
4. list of ingredients
5. clear, wobbly dessert

Now, unscramble the circled letters. If you did the puzzle correctly, the circled letters when put in the right order and added to the one below, will tell what you are just before dinner. _ _ _ g _ _

13

7. Care for Some Jellied Flgmzx?

   Guess who's coming for supper tonight? A being from Mars. It has just arrived in its flying saucer and it insists on making supper for us. What recipe will it use?

   Write a story telling about the supper the Martian made. You might tell what it cooked and how it did the work.

A Tricky Ending

				stumble
				axle
				cradle

popsicle	mammal	double	turtle	gentle
personal	trial	settle	circle	settlement
royal	idle	eagle	kettle	simple

You can't always rely on the sound of a word when you are spelling, as you can see by the words in this unit. Some of the words end in **al**, others end in **le**, but both endings sound the same.

1. (a) Write the word in the list that ends in **al** and has more than two syllables. After the word write the number of syllables it contains.
    (b) Write the words that end in **al** and have two syllables.
    (c) Make a list of all the words in the list that end in **le**. Write the number of syllables after each one.

2. (a) Which **al** word is a complete word when the **al** is removed?
   (b) **al** is often used as a suffix. Add this suffix to **nature** and **centre**. (Remember to make a change in the base before adding **al**.)
   (c) Which word in the list is formed from **try**?

3. (a) Which two **le** words name animals?
   (b) Write **settlement** and the word in the list which is its base.
   (c) Write another word having the same base that means a person who settles in a certain place.

4. (a) Write **simple**, **double**, and **idle**. Make new words by dropping the **e** from each word and adding **y**.
   (b) Make a list of the words that have double letters. Make a title for your list in which you use the word **double**.

5. Write the word in the list that means
   (a) a large bird with a hooked beak.
   (b) animal whose young are born alive.
   (c) something perfectly round.
   (d) fruit-flavoured ice on a stick.

6. The "Sometimes" game: find words in the list that go with the clues below.
   (a) sometimes used to describe the Queen, her husband, and their children (the _____ family)
   (b) sometimes used as the name of a kind of drum
   (c) sometimes called a tortoise
   (d) sometimes used in a courtroom (a person is on _____)

7. You have a summer job helping at the local zoo. Right now you are just on trial. You have to prove you can do the job. Your first test is simple. Feed the eagle and wash the turtle. Or was it to wash the eagle and feed the turtle? Write a story about your first day on the job.

Keep a personal spelling list. Put in it the words that give you trouble and words that you especially want to remember.

5   Words About Clothing

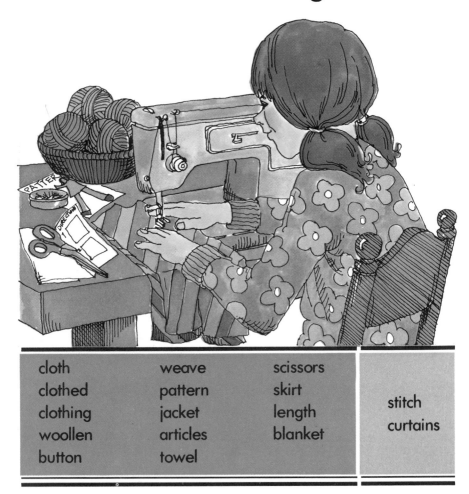

cloth	weave	scissors	
clothed	pattern	skirt	stitch
clothing	jacket	length	curtains
woollen	articles	blanket	
button	towel		

1. (a) Write the first three words in the list, marking the **o** as long or short in each word. Write another word that is formed from the same base word.
   (b) Under the heading **Articles of Clothing** write the names of articles of clothing that are found in the list.
   (c) In grammar, what name is given to the words **a**, **an**, **the**?

2. (a) Write the word **scissors**. Underline the double **s**. What sound does this double letter make?
   (b) Circle the silent letter in **scissors**.

3. (a) Write the word **weave**. Now write the **ing** form of the word.
   (b) What is the past form of **weave**?

4. (a) Which word in the list is formed from the word **long**?
   (b) Write a word formed from **wide** that ends with the same two letters as the word you just wrote.

5. Use the word **skirt** in a sentence that shows its usual meaning. Tell what **skirt** means in each sentence below. Use a dictionary if you need help.
    They live on the outskirts of the city.
    The salesman tried to skirt the issue of price.

6. (a) Which words in the list contain these names: Jack, Pat, Len, Art?
   (b) Write the plural forms of the words in the list that can be made plural.
   (c) Which word in the list is already plural? Write its singular form.
   (d) Which word may be either singular or plural?

7. Some of our words about clothing have interesting stories. Read the stories below and write the word that you think each tells about.
   (a) This word is formed from the French word **blanc**, meaning **white**. Long ago, the word meant a white woollen cloth.
   (b) This word is formed from an old word that meant **wash**. The word now means something you use after washing.

8. This monkey has just had a lot of fun playing at being human. What do you think has happened? What might happen next? Write an exciting and funny story about the monkey's adventures.

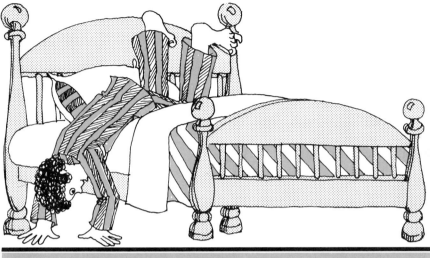

knowledge	recipe	length	imagine
league	kitchen	blanket	refrigerator
lose	saucer	pattern	simple
losing	double	scissors	settlement
practice	personal	signal	articles
sausage	circle	strikes	clothing

Follow the steps for learning to spell a word.

1. (a) Sounds of **g**. Make a chart on your page like the one below. Put the words with **g** in the proper columns.

hard (gun)	soft (gem)	silent	**ng**

   (b) List the words that contain a vowel pair. Circle the vowel pair and tell the sound that each makes.

2. Write
   (a) the words that end in **al** or **le**.
   (b) the word that ends in **les**.
   (c) the word that ends in **le** plus a suffix.
   (d) the word that ends in an **e** that is not silent.

3. (a) List the words that contain the letter **n** with a consonant either just before or just after the **n**.
   (b) What is the base word of **strikes**?
   (c) What is the plural form of **practice**?
   (d) Write the base word of **losing**. What is the sound of **s** in **losing**? How was the base word changed before **ing** was added?

4. Which word ...?
   (a) contains 4 **s**'s
   (b) is formed from **long**
   (c) means a room in which cooking is done
   (d) means very easy
   (e) begins like **circus**
   (f) contains 4 **r**'s

5. Write the words in the list that are formed from these base words: **know**, **sign**, **image**, **person**, **clothe**.

6. Which words mean ...?
   (a) a model or guide for making something
   (b) directions for making something to eat
   (c) a cover
   (d) a variety of objects
   (e) something done to improve skill

7. Write **scissors** on your page as it is written below. Use each letter of **scissors** as the first letter to write another word from the list. The blanks tell you how many letters are in each word. Find the word for **o** in Unit 3.

   S _ _ _ _ _ _
   C _ _ _ _ _ _ _
   I _ _ _ _ _ _
   S _ _ _ _ _
   S _ _ _ _ _
   O _ _ _
   R _ _ _ _ _ _ _ _ _ _
   S _ _ _ _ _ _

1. (a) Which words in the list contain these smaller words: **art**, **pat**, **ledge**, **itch**, **blank**, **rat**?
   (b) Which words contain double consonants?
   (c) In which words is the letter **c** sounded as /s/?

2. Which word names
   (a) something to eat?
   (b) a place where food is kept cool?
   (c) something put under a cup?
   (d) a group of teams?
   (e) to make a sign?

3. (a) Put the words in Column 3 in alphabetical order.
   (b) Add **ing** to these words: **imagine**, **double**, **circle**. How must you change the base word?
   (c) Write **refrigerator**. Circle the last two **r**'s and the letter before each one.

4. Write **imagine** after the letter of each item that you would have to imagine. Write **knowledge** after each of the ones that you have knowledge of.
   (a) life on Venus
   (b) how your bed feels
   (c) how to get from your house to school
   (d) where you will be ten years from today
   (e) how you did on your last spelling test

5. Names in Words
   Write the words from the list that contain these names.
   The blanks show how many letters you must add.
   - _ _ _ _ _ _ E D _ _   • S _ _ _ A L
   - K _ _ _ _ E N   • _ _ _ _ _ _ _ A L
   - P _ A _ T _ _ _

For Good Spellers

1. (a) **Refrigerator** has one prefix and three suffixes. Write
       refrigerator and its root.
   (b) Use the root to write a word that means very cold.
   (c) Write three other words you know that end in **or**.

2. (a) Add these suffixes to **imagine**: **ation**, **ary**, **able**. Use
       each new word in a sentence.
   (b) Which words in the list are the opposites of **winning**,
       difficult, **width**, **public**, **ignorance**?

3. Write
   (a) **league** and at least three other words that end in **ue**.
   (b) **articles** and at least two other words that end in **cles**.
   (c) **length** and three other words that end in **th**.

4. **Strike** usually means **to hit**. What does **strike** mean in
   baseball? How do you think it came to have that meaning?

5. **Double** means twice as much, so is related to two. Which words are related in the same way to **one**, **three**, **four**, and **five**?

6. Criss-Cross
   Write **refrigerator** as it is written below. Be sure to put the correct number of spaces in each criss-crossing arm. Use the clues to fill in the criss-cross. All the words except the first are in the list.

   Clues
   1. countries other than your own (adjective)
   2. hits
   3. pretend
   4. group of teams
   5. ring
   6. belonging to you

7　The Book of Words

A dictionary is one of the most useful books in your school. It is also one of the most interesting. As you study words, you find that each word has a story of its own. Many word stories are told in other places in this spelling book. Some dictionaries tell the histories of words. Even those that don't, contain interesting information. Learn to use a dictionary quickly and accurately.

flakes	oar	stool	raisin
itch	aerial	rise	acquainted
ashes	ticket	swept	spider
	parka	missed	

| drown | calves | yolk |

- Order of Words
1. (a) Which word in the list would be closest to the beginning of a dictionary? Which would be closest to the end? Which would be near the middle?
   (b) List the words in the first two columns in the order they would come in a dictionary.

- Guide Words
2. (a) If the guide words on a page are **soft - string**, which words in the list would be found on that page?

(b) Write **raisin - rice**. If these were guide words, list three other words you know that would be on that page.

- Base Words
3. To find a word in a dictionary, you must usually look for the base form. Which words in the list are not in their base form? Write each of them and beside each write its base form.

- Meanings
4. (a) A **spider** is an insect. Use a dictionary to find another meaning of **spider**. Write a sentence to show this new meaning.
   (b) **Rise** means **to go up**. Find three other meanings of **rise** and write a sentence for each one.

- Parts of Speech
5. (a) Make a list of these words in alphabetical order: **oar**, **ticket**, **flakes**, **parka**, **itch**.
   (b) Look up each of the words in (a) and beside each write the part of speech it may be. Look carefully. Some may be used as more than one part of speech.

6. Invent-a-Word
   Dictionaries show the meaning of a word by explaining it. Sometimes the word is used in a sentence. Sometimes a picture is used to help describe the word.

parka (pär'kə)n [Aleut, skin, outer garment, fr. Russ., pelt, fr. Yurak]1: a hooded fur pullover garment for arctic wear. 2: a fabric pullover or jacket for sports or military wear.

a parka

Invent three brand-new words of your own. Use one or all three of the ways a dictionary uses to explain the meanings of your words. Share your words with your friends. Perhaps you could make a class dictionary of the words you invent.

Remember to keep your personal spelling list up to date.

8 Two Uncommon Letters

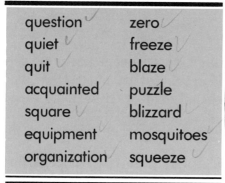

question	zero
quiet	freeze
quit	blaze
acquainted	puzzle
square	blizzard
equipment	mosquitoes
organization	squeeze

The letter **e** is the most frequently used letter in the alphabet. The letters **q** and **z** are among the least common letters. These two letters sometimes cause problems in handwriting. Be sure you write **qu** and **z** carefully.

1. (a) Write the words in the list that have the combination **qui**. In which of these words is the **i** long? Write that word again.
   (b) Which two words in the list rhyme?
   (c) Write the word that is in the plural. Beside it, write the singular form. Check the spelling of the singular in a dictionary. What is the last letter of the singular form?
   (d) Write a sentence using the word **blizzard** in which you tell two things about a winter storm.

2. (a) Which two letters in **acquainted** give a /k/ sound? Write **acquainted** and circle these two letters.
   (b) Write the base word of **acquainted**. Make new words by adding **ing** and **ance** to the base word.
   (c) Write the numerals 1 to 5. After the numerals which are in a square below, write **square**.

3. (a) What happens to the vowel sound when we add **e** to **quit**? Write both **quit** and the same word with **e** added. Now add **ing** to **quit**. What happens to the final **t**?

   (b) Add **er**, **est**, and **ly** to **quiet**. Name something that is quiet and tell of something that is quieter. Use **quietly** in a sentence that tells something that you do quietly.

4. (a) Write **equipment**. Draw a box around the suffix. Add **ed** to the base word. What happens to **p**?

   (b) What is the base word of **question**? Add the prefixes **in**, **con**, and **re** to the base. Use the new words in sentences that show you know what they mean.

   (c) Write an answer to this question in which you use two words from the list: What happens to water at zero degrees Celsius?

5. (a) Write **organization**. Write the form of this word to which **ation** was added. Now write a sentence in which you show that you know the meaning of **organization**.

   (b) Use a dictionary if you need to to find two meanings of **blaze**. Write two sentences to show these two meanings.

   (c) Write **puzzle**. Make new words by changing the **p** to **g**, then to **m**.

6. Crazy Questions
   Here are some answers, for a change. You can have some fun by making up crazy questions to fit the answers. Write the word **question** before each question you write. For example: Answer: He was wearing rubber boots.
   Question: Why did the elephant surprise you?

   (a) Answer: He ate bacon and eggs for breakfast.

   (b) Answer: She won the tennis championship.

   (c) Answer: They were squeezing lemons.

   (d) Answer: It was square.

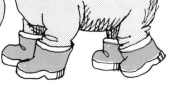

9 Words About School

library	memory	choose	studying
audience	paragraph	equipped	objectives
assignment	topic	projector	alphabet
	review	speech	dictionary

elementary texts

1. (a) Where are the people in the picture studying?
   (b) Divide **library** into syllables. How many syllables does it have?
   (c) Write **library** again. Circle the two **r**'s. Make a new word by adding the suffix **an** to **library**. What change must you make in the base word?

2. Answer these questions using the words in bold type and at least one other word from the list in your answer.
   (a) What is a good place to find information for an **assignment**?
   (b) Why should you have clear **objectives** before you start work on an assignment?
   (c) Why might a school be **equipped** with a **projector**?
   (d) Name two kinds of books that are arranged in the same order as the **alphabet**.

3. (a) Which two words in the list have the **ph** combination?
   (b) List three other words you know that end, like **paragraph**, in **graph**.
   (c) Write **audience**. Make a new word by adding **ble** to the base. What does the new word mean? Add the prefix **in** to the new word and make another new word. What is its meaning?

Don't forget the steps for learning to spell a word.

5 Practise
4 Check
3 Write
2 Think
1 Look

   (d) The word **assignment** has both a prefix and a suffix. Write the base word. Add only the prefix and write the new word. Add another prefix to the new word to get a word that means **not assigned**.

4. Use the words in bold type in your answers to these questions. Use other words from the list if you can.
   (a) What might be a good **topic** for a **speech**?
   (b) Why must a speaker think about the **audience**?
   (c) Why must a speaker have a good **memory**?

5. (a) Write **studying** and its base word.
   (b) Add the suffix **ed** to the base. How must you change the base word?
   (c) Write **memory**. Make a new word by adding the suffix **ize**. How must you change the base word?
   (d) The root of **memory** is **memor**. What other word do you know that is formed from the same root?
   (e) Write **review** and its base word. What does the prefix **re** mean?

6. Write **speech** on your page as it is written below. Use each letter in **speech** as the first letter in a word that has something to do with school. The first three words can be found in the list. You must find the others yourself.

   S
   P
   E
   E
   C
   H

7. Al Phabet and Dick Shunary
   Al Phabet and Dick Shunary are two people who take a lot of abuse at school. Suppose Al and Dick were real people. What problems does Al Phabet have? What really bothers Dick Shunary?

   Write a story about one or both of these characters. Maybe you can give life to some other school objects too.

You Speak Many Languages

theatre	per cent	essay	museum	petroleum
index	wieners	beauty	roses	auditorium
camera	restaurant	prison	liberty	

You may not realize it, but you know something about several languages besides English. The English language has borrowed words from many other languages, sometimes without any change in spelling and sometimes with only a small change. For example, **beauty** and **liberty** are from the French words **beauté** and **liberté**. **Index** and **camera** are from Latin words that are spelled exactly the same.

Some dictionaries tell you the stories of some of the words in the list. There are also books about interesting word stories.

1. (a) Write **camera**. The Latin word **camera** means a small room. Write a sentence using the word **camera** in which you tell what part of a camera is like a small room.
   (b) The word **index** has two plural forms. Write the singular form and then use a dictionary to find the two plural forms. Which finger is your index finger? How is **index** related in meaning to **indicate**?
   (c) What does **per cent** mean? These words are a short form of **per centum**. Write in words 80%, 10%.

2. (a) Write the words in the list that end in **eum**.
   (b) In a sentence, name three things that you might find on display in a museum.
   (c) Tell three things that are made from petroleum. Write your answer in a sentence.

3. Use words from the list to answer these questions.
   (a) How is the auditorium in your school used?
   (b) Why would you go to a theatre?
   (c) What is your favourite restaurant?

4. (a) **Essay** is from a French word that means **try**. How is the English meaning related to the French? Write a title using the word **essay**.
   (b) What is the plural of **essay**?

5. (a) Write the singular forms, **beauty** and **liberty**.
   (b) Now write the plural forms. What change do you make in the base word when you write the plural?

6. Wieners are named after a famous city in Austria. If you find the name of the city you may find it easier to spell **wieners**. Write **wieners**. Use a dictionary or other reference book to find the name of the city.

7. Some Riddles
   The answers are words in the list.
   (a) I have keys and bars but I am not music.
   (b) People have fought and died for me because they want to be free.
   (c) I make pictures using light and film.
   (d) We are used as gifts and decorations. Many people grow us as a hobby.

Stories in Food

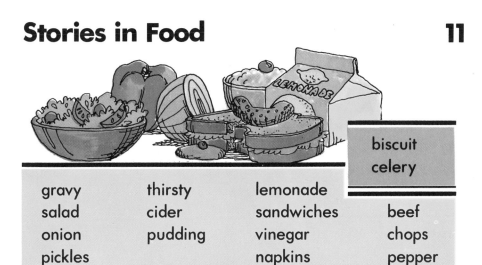

			biscuit
			celery
gravy	thirsty	lemonade	
salad	cider	sandwiches	beef
onion	pudding	vinegar	chops
pickles		napkins	pepper

Many of the words we use to name foods have interesting stories. For example, the word **onion** in Latin means **pearl** as well as **onion**. Our words **union** and **unite** are from the same root. Why do you think the Romans thought of onions and pearls as being alike?

1. (a) Write **thirsty**. Now list two things from the words above that you might drink if you were thirsty.
   (b) Write the names of two things that you would eat if you were hungry.
   (c) Which word names a spice?

2. (a) The Earl of Sandwich was so busy playing cards that he would not stop for dinner. He ordered that some beef be placed between two slices of bread and brought to him. That meal is now named after him. Write the word in the list that names his invention.

   (b) Write the names of the foods in the list that you might use in making one of the things you named in (a).

3. (a) Which word names the kind of meat that we get from cattle?
   (b) Which word names the juice that we get from meat?
   (c) Which word means either to cut with an axe or a slice of meat, especially pork or lamb?
   (d) Which word means cucumbers preserved in vinegar?

4. (a) Write the word **pepper**. How is the word **pep** related in meaning to **pepper**?
   (b) Add another word to **pepper** to make a compound word that names a flavour of gum or candy.

5. (a) Write the words that name things you might take with you on a picnic.
   (b) Which word names something you might have for dessert?

6. Can You Guess the Words That Have These Stories?
   Here are four stories about words in the list. Write the word that each story tells about.
   (a) This word comes from the same root as **apron**, which used to be called **a napron**.
   (b) This word comes from the same root as **salt**, the Latin word **salsus**.
   (c) This word comes from a French root that meant **sour wine**. The first part of the word is almost like **wine**.
   (d) This word comes from an Arabic word, **lima**, from which we also get the word **lime**.

7. Draw up a menu for a meal using some of the foods named in the list, and others you like.

Take Two

In making movies, if something is not quite right the first time, the scene is shot again. The second shot is "Take 2". Take a second shot of these words to be sure you know them well.

acquainted	puzzle	wieners	blizzard
missed	camera	ticket	studying
equipment	pickles	sandwiches	audience
paragraph	choose	organization	dictionary
gravy	square	assignment	pudding
beauty	review	auditorium	mosquitoes
raisin			

1. (a) Put in alphabetical order all the words in the list that begin with **a**, **b**, or **c**.
   (b) Which words in the list are plurals?
   (c) Give the singular form of each word you wrote in (b).
   (d) Which words in the list contain more than three syllables?

2. Write
   (a) **acquainted**, its base word, and new words made by adding **ance** and **ing** to the base.
   (b) **auditorium** and two other words formed from the root **audi**.
   (c) **paragraph** and two other words that end in **graph**.
   (d) each of the five words that contain the three vowels, **a**, **e**, and **u**.

3. Which words in the list were formed from these base words: **miss**, **study**, **view**, **equip**, **organ**?

4. Which words have these meanings . . . ?
   (a) juice from meat
   (b) problem often done for fun
   (c) dried grape
   (d) soft cooked food, often a dessert
   (e) card or piece of paper that lets you in to see a hockey game or gives you a chance in a draw
   (f) select
   (g) small biting insects

5. (a) Only four words in the list have a long **a** sound. Write the four words.
   (b) One word contains both the first and last letters of the alphabet. Which word is it?
   (c) Which words in the list name things you could eat?
   (d) Which words name things you could read, write, or draw?
   (e) One word contains both the second and the second last letter of the alphabet. Which word is it?

6. The clues below are for small words that are contained in words in the list. For each clue, write the small word and the list word.
   (a) not a hit, but a _____
   (b) select or choose
   (c) the _____ -tock of a clock
   (d) found on beaches
   (e) signal

7. Forced Choice
   Sometimes you can be very creative when you are forced to think in a certain way. Write a sentence for each set of words below. Use all three words in an interesting way. You may change the order of words if you wish.
   (a) assignment . . . gravy . . . mosquitoes
   (b) wieners . . . blizzard . . . square
   (c) paragraph . . . raisin . . . puzzle
   (d) review . . . sandwiches . . . beauty

Are you using the study steps for learning to spell?

1. (a) Which words in the list end in the suffix **ed** or **ment**?
    (b) Write the base word for each word you wrote in (a).
    (c) Which words in the list contain double consonants?

2. (a) List the words that you would find in a dictionary between the words **pan** and **square**.
    (b) Which words in the list end with a vowel sound?
    (c) Which words contain these smaller words: **toes, study, quaint, organ, be**?

3. Which Words?
    (a) contain three vowels together
    (b) contain three **a**'s
    (c) contain seven consonants
    (d) begin and end with the same letter

4. (a) Put into alphabetical order: **choose, square, review, wieners, ticket**.
    (b) Which words in the list contain the sound /k/? Circle the letter or letters that make the sound.

5. Which Word Am I?
    (a) I need bread and something in between.
    (b) Drop my **ing**, add **le**, and I am all wet.
    (c) Change my first letter to **t** and I am what a feather does.
    (d) Change my **re** to **sh** and I am a vegetable, a game, or a tight fit.
    (e) Add **p** before me and I mean something seen beforehand.

1. (a) Make as many new words as you can from **puzzle** by changing only the first letter.
    (b) Start with the first three letters of **square** and make as many new words as you can.
    (c) Write three other words that begin, like **paragraph**, with **para**.

2. (a) The root of **organization** is **organ**. Add prefixes or suffixes to make five new words from the root.
    (b) **Wieners** are named after Vienna. Name three other foods that are named after cities.

3. (a) The base word of **dictionary** is **diction**. Find the meaning of **diction**.
    (b) What is the meaning of each of these words: **jurisdiction, benediction, malediction, verdict**?
    (c) What does each word in (b) have to do with speaking?

4. What does each of these words have to do with writing: **autograph, photograph, telegraph, graphic**?

5. Headlines
    Write a short newspaper report that might appear under each headline on this newspaper page. If you wish, make up a humorous headline of your own and write the story for it too.

13 Two-in-One

Many words in the English language have been formed by joining two shorter words. For example, **photo** and **graph**, two Greek words that mean **light** and **writing** are put together to form our word **photograph**. Have you ever thought of a photograph, or a snapshot (also a compound word), as something **written** on a film with **light**?

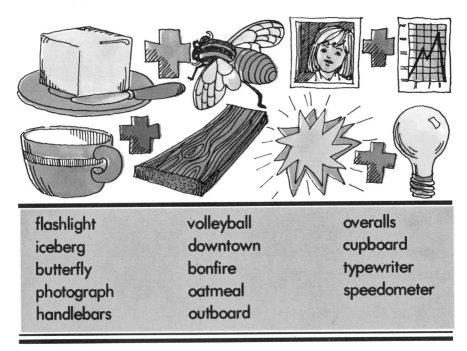

flashlight	volleyball	overalls
iceberg	downtown	cupboard
butterfly	bonfire	typewriter
photograph	oatmeal	speedometer
handlebars	outboard	

1. (a) Write each word in the list.
   (b) Draw a line between the two words in each compound word.

2. Write answers to these questions using words from the list.
   (a) In what game is a ball hit back and forth over a net?
   (b) What may be used to measure speed?
   (c) What is a floating mountain of ice called?
   (d) What is the central part of a city called?
   (e) What do you call a motor placed on the outside of a boat?

3. (a) Most of the words in the list are usually nouns, but some of them may be used as other parts of speech as well. Make up sentences in which you use **volleyball**, **photograph**, and **typewriter** as adjectives.

   (b) Write **speedometer**. What word ends the same way and means an instrument used to measure temperature?

   (c) Write (i) **flashlight**, (ii) **photograph**, and (iii) **cupboard**. Make new compound words by using the second part of each with the word with the matching number: (i) **search**, (ii) **auto**, (iii) **over**.

4. Use a dictionary to help you with these questions.

   (a) Use **oatmeal** in a sentence that explains why it means what it does.

   (b) Why do you think **overalls** is a useful compound word? Use the word in your answer.

   (c) Write **cupboard**. Your dictionary may have several meanings of **board**. Which meaning was used in making the compound word **cupboard**?

   (d) Use your imagination to explain how the word **butterfly** got its name.

5. Several of the compound words in the list are quite modern. They have been put together to describe new things or inventions. Write the words that you think are recent additions to the language.

6. New inventions require new names. Make up some new inventions. Tell what each of your inventions does and give it a name that is a brand-new word. For example: I've just invented a machine that frightens dogs. I call it a **bow-wow wower**. I also have a loop of rope that I use to catch wild moose. It is called a **loose-moose noose**.

14 Don't Shun -tion

The suffix **tion** sounds like the word "shun". But it is a very important suffix to know. So do not shun it.

hesitate

association
direction
position
prepare
pollution
education
mention
object
attention
section
prevent
decoration
instruction
invitation

1. Make two columns on your page. Put the heading **Verbs** at the top of one, and the heading **Nouns** at the top of the other. Now put each of the following words in the verb column, and beside each write the noun in the list that is formed from it.

    associate, **educate**, **decorate**, **pollute**, **direct**, **instruct**, **attend**, **invite**

2. (a) Write all the two-syllable words in the list that end in **tion**.
    (b) Now make a list of the three-syllable words that end in **tion**.
    (c) Which words in the list have four syllables?
    (d) Which word has five syllables?

3. (a) Write the words in the list that do not end in **tion**.
    (b) What part of speech is each word you wrote in (a)?
    (c) Make these words into nouns by adding **ion** or **tion**.

(d) In one of the words you must make a change in the root word, and the suffix must be **ation**. Write that word again.

4. (a) Make new words from **prepare**. Add a prefix and a final **d** to get a word that means **not ready**. Then change the prefix **pre** to **com**, and write the new word in a sentence that shows its meaning.

   (b) Add the prefix **op** to **position**. Write the new word in a sentence that shows its meaning. Write two other words you know that contain the root **posit**.

   (c) Write a command in which you use the word **attention**.

5. (a) Make up two sentences using the word **object**. In one sentence use it as a noun, in the other as a verb. How does the accent in **object** change depending on its use?

   (b) The words **association** and **society** both have the same root, **soc**. Tell how the two words are related in meaning. Use a dictionary if you need help. (Hint: the Latin word **socius** means **friend**.)

6. Word Pictures

   You can make a word into a picture by writing the letters in a certain shape or by adding some shading or a few lines. Think about the sound of all or part of the word, or about its meaning, or about words related to it. Here are two word pictures. Use two or three other words in the list to make word pictures of your own. **Decoration** and **instruction** might be good ones to try.

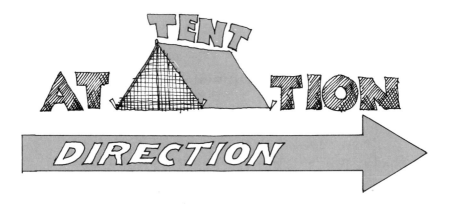

15 Some Sports Words

baseball		motto	lacrosse
guard	rink	hockey	lose
instructor	soccer	league	losing
basketball	tennis	excellent	practice

1. (a) Which sports named in the list are played with a ball?
    (b) One word in the list names a sport and another word
        tells where that sport is played. Write both words.
    (c) Which word names something that is needed if you are
        to be good in sports?

2. Which words mean
    (a) one who teaches?
    (b) opposite of **win**, **winning**?
    (c) much better than average?
    (d) defend?

3. Write
    (a) the words in the list that are compounds.
    (b) the words formed from **instruct**, **excel**.

(c) a word with three short vowels.

(d) a word that starts like **guest**.

4. Write the name of the sport that each group of words below refers to.
   - (a) net, racket, love
   - (b) net, goaltender, ice
   - (c) net, goaltender, ball
   - (d) indoors, winter, large ball
   - (e) outdoors, summer, small ball

5. Answer these questions using the words in heavy type and other words from the list.
   - (a) In what sport is one position called **guard**?
   - (b) In what sports can you get **practice** by playing against the school wall?
   - (c) What is the full name of the **league** called the NHL?

6. Common words such as **icing**, **love**, **steal**, **dribble**, and **heading** have different meanings when used in sports. For each statement below, tell the sport it refers to and explain what the word in heavy type means.
   - (a) They are **icing** the puck too often.
   - (b) She won the game forty-**love**.
   - (c) He is going to **steal** home.
   - (d) **Dribble**, then pass.
   - (e) He will pass the ball by **heading** it.

7. Picking Up the Leftovers
   Make a list of all the silent letters that are contained in words in the list. You should have thirteen silent letters. For double-letter sounds, count the second letter as silent. Now, use the silent letters to complete the words below, and write the words on your own paper. The clues give you hints about the words.

d __ f __ __ __ __	position in hockey
__ __ w n	a kind of tennis
f __ t __ r __	what is to come
__ i __ __	murder

16 A Pair of Prefixes

Look at the words on the left. **Con** or **com** is a Latin prefix. It often means **along with** or **together**. A **convention** is a coming together, **con** meaning **together** and **vention** from a Latin word meaning **come**.

Now look at the words on the right. **Ex** is also a Latin prefix, usually meaning **out of** or **from**, or **thoroughly**.

compass
contain
control
complete
continent
convention

example
executive
exhibit
exhibition
excellent
exercise
excitement

contour   correspond

1. (a) Which form of the prefix **con** or **com** is used before the letter **p**? Which is used before the letter **t**?
   (b) Write the words that begin with the prefix **com**.
   (c) Use a dictionary to find two other words that begin with the prefix **com** followed by **p**, and add the two words to your list.

2. (a) Both **contain** and **continent** come from the Latin word that means **hold together** or **hold within**. Write **contain** and **continent**. Tell how you think they are still related in meaning.
   (b) Add the suffix **er** to **contain** and the suffix **al** to **continent**. Use each new word in a sentence that shows you know what it means.
   (c) Add **ed** and **er** to **control**. What change must you make in the base word?

3. (a) Remove the prefix from **convention** and make new words by adding the prefixes **in** and **pre**.
   (b) Remove the suffix from the two words you wrote in (a) to get two new words.
   (c) Which words in the list mean: finished, a display, a large land mass, a large gathering, an instrument for finding direction?

4. (a) List in alphabetical order the words that have the prefix **ex**. Underline the prefix of each of these words.
   (b) Drop the suffix of **excitement** and change the prefix to **in**. Find the new word in a dictionary and write its meaning.

5. (a) Write the verbs that can be formed from **excellent**, **exhibition**, and **executive**.
   (b) Which words in the list were formed from these words: **excel**, **convene**, **excite**?

6. Make a Word
   Below you are given two definitions. To make a word, follow these steps:
   (i) write a word for the definition in Column A;
   (ii) add to that word one of the prefixes studied in the list.
   (iii) The new word must match the definition in Column B. The first one is done for you. The last two answers are not in the list.

   (pass — compass)

A	B
to go by	instrument to tell direction
enough	a sample
examination	a race or competition
sit for a picture	show, display

17 Words to Build With

promote	offered	regular	defend
subway	disappear	returned	different
provide	opposite	department	disappointed
			immediately

defence
absorb

Each word in this list can be used as a building block for other words. Take **provide** as an example. It comes from the Latin words **pro**, ahead, and **videre**, to see. From **provide** you can build **provident**, **providence**, and **provision**. Remove the prefix **pro** from **provision** and you have **vision**. From that you can make **television, division**, and many others.

The exercises in this unit will help you build new words. You will find a dictionary that gives origins of words a big help.

1. (a) Two words in the list have the root **fer**, which means to carry or to bear. Write the two words.
   (b) Write two other words you know that have the same root. The prefixes **con** and **pre** may help.

2. (a) Write **department**. Remove the prefix and the suffix. What is the base word?
   (b) List three other words formed from the same base.
   (c) What other word in the list has the same prefix? Make a new word from it by changing the prefix.
   (d) What noun is formed from the verb **defend**? What adjective is formed from it?

3. (a) Which words in the list have the prefix **dis**?
   (b) Make new words from **disappear**. First, add a suffix. Next, remove the prefix and add a different suffix.
   (c) Write **disappointed**. Circle the base word.
   (d) Build at least four other words from the base **point**.

4. (a) Write **subway**. Use a dictionary to find the meaning of the prefix **sub**. Give two other words that have this prefix.
   (b) What is the base of **subway**? Make new words from the base by adding **high**, **side**, **breeze**, **walk**.
   (c) Write **returned**. What is its base? Combine the base with **over**, **table**, and **coat** to make new words.

5. Write
   (a) **opposite**; from its root make two new words.
   (b) **immediately**; the root means **middle**; write two other words that have the root **medi**.
   (c) **regular**; the root means **rule**; circle the root; make two new words from the same root.
   (d) another word in the list that has the same prefix as **provide**. What is the root of the word you just wrote? Make three new words from this root.

6. The Case of the Missing Guest
   Write a short mystery story that uses at least four of these key words, in any order you wish.
   ... disappeared ... subway ... immediately ... disappointed ... defend

18　One More Time

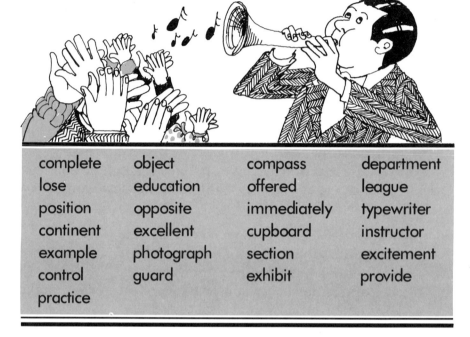

complete	object	compass	department
lose	education	offered	league
position	opposite	immediately	typewriter
continent	excellent	cupboard	instructor
example	photograph	section	excitement
control	guard	exhibit	provide
practice			

1. (a) Make a chart with these prefixes as headings: **ex, com, con**. Under each heading put the words from the list that belong there.
   (b) Write these suffixes as headings for a chart: **tion, ent, ment**. Under each heading place the words that belong in that column.

2. (a) Two words in the list have the root **posit**. Which words are they? Write three other words formed from the same root.
   (b) Which words in the list are compound words? Circle the silent letters in each one.
   (c) One word has four vowels, but only one syllable. Which word is it?

3. (a) Which words were formed from these base words: **educate, excel, offer, immediate, instruct**?
   (b) Which word contains one hard **c** and one soft **c**?
   (c) What part of speech is the word you wrote in (b)?
   (d) What is the verb form of the word you wrote in (b)?

4. One Who . . .
   Add **er** or **or** to words in the list to get words with these meanings.
   (a) one who loses
   (b) one who objects
   (c) one who photographs
   (d) one who provides
   (e) one who exhibits

5. (a) Write **guard**. Add the suffix **ian**. Use the new word in a sentence to show its meaning.
   (b) Which words are the opposites of **unfinished, received, agree, same**?
   (c) Which word contains all the vowels?

6. Match Them
   The base words of two words in the list are related in meaning to two other words in the list. One pair of words is related to **give**. The other pair is related to **part**. Write the two pairs of words.

7. Word Square
   Use the clues to fill in the word square. All the words except the last are in the list.

   Clues
   1. Across: helps you to find north
   1. Down: hold back or keep down
   2. Down: a part of
   2. Across: a portable light in a case to protect it from wind or rain

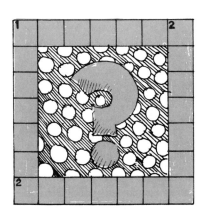

Remember to keep a personal list with the correct spelling of words you want to use.

1. (a) Which words in the list begin with two or more consonants?
   (b) Which words contain double consonants?
   (c) Only two words have more than three syllables. Which are they?

2. Which word ... ?
   (a) names something you use to keep from getting lost
   (b) names something that might be used to write a letter
   (c) means **right away**
   (d) names a large land mass such as North America
   (e) means a part of something
   (f) begins and ends with the same pair of letters

3. (a) Add **ing** to these words: **complete, lose, provide, guard, exhibit.** How must you change the base word for the first three words?
   (b) Write the plural forms of **continent, object, compass, league, cupboard.**

4. (a) Add the prefix **un** to these words: **offered, provided, guarded, excited.**
   (b) What is the meaning of the prefix **un**?

5. Criss-Cross
   Make two criss-crosses on your page like the ones below. Be sure to put the correct number of spaces in each. Use the clues to find the words that fit in the criss-crosses.
   (a) 1. finished   (b) 1. secretary's helper
       2. a lost person's helper   2. without any delay

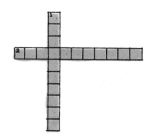

1. (a) **Complete** is from a word which means **filled** (**pletum**). Use the prefix **re** or **de** or a suffix and make three new words from the same root.
    (b) Make five new words by adding prefixes or suffixes to the root of **provide**.
    (c) The root of **object** is **ject**, to throw. Write three other words from the same root.

2. Use a dictionary to find the meanings of **league** in the sentences below.
    He plays in a professional football league.
    They are in league with the enemy.

3. What's the difference ...
    (a) between a **section** and a **department**?
    (b) between **offer** and **provide**?
    (c) between **education** and **training**?

4. (a) List three other words besides **teacher** and **instructor** that could name a person who teaches.
    (b) Give three other words that are similar in meaning to **exhibit**.

5. The last letter of each word is the first letter of the word that follows it. Use the clues to find the words in the list.
    (a) what a baby-sitter should do with children
    (b) what a baby-sitter should not do with children
    (c) what a baby-sitter should set for children
    (d) what baby-sitting is when a baby-sitter doesn't have (a)

19 Words About Government

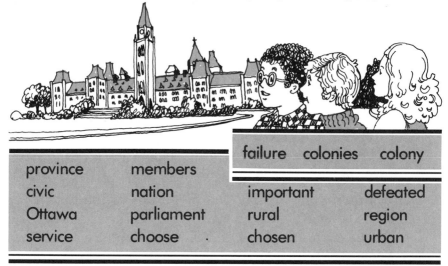

		failure	colonies	colony
province	members			
civic	nation	important		defeated
Ottawa	parliament	rural		region
service	choose	chosen		urban

1. Answer these questions using the word in bold type and at least one other word from the list.
   (a) Where does the federal **parliament** meet?
   (b) What is each political **region** of Canada called?
   (c) What name is given to people who have been **chosen** to sit in parliament?

2. The names of cities are **civic** names. The names of provinces are **provincial** names. Write the letters (a) to (f), and after each letter write **civic** or **provincial**, whichever is correct for each of these places:
   (a) Winnipeg, (b) Manitoba, (c) Hamilton, (d) Montreal, (e) British Columbia, (f) Halifax.

3. (a) Which two words in the list are different forms of the same word?
   (b) Add the suffix **ing** to **choose**. What change must you make in the base word?
   (c) Write the word that ends in **ed**. Beside it write its base word.
   (d) Add a prefix to the base word you wrote in (c) to get a word that means **not defeated**.
   (e) Which two words in the list refer to something about a city?

4. Use the words in bold type in your answer to each question.
   (a) In which **province** do you live?
   (b) In which geographic **region** do you live?
   (c) What **important** jobs are you **chosen** to do?
   (d) What are three **services** that young people can do for their country?

5. Write the letters (a) to (f). After each letter write **rural** or **urban** to name the area where you would be most likely to see the thing named:
   (a) a large farm, (b) an apartment building, (c) a streetcar, (d) a tractor, (e) a traffic jam, (f) an orchard.

6. Ottawa Word Search
   There are nine other words from the list in this puzzle. Write them on your own paper in the same places you find them in the puzzle. You will need a square eleven spaces by eleven.

S	A	B	E	T	E	O	R	F	Z	Y
E	K	M	E	S	T	B	U	I	U	O
R	I	M	O	F	C	L	R	G	P	X
V	R	O	T	T	A	W	A	I	R	T
I	H	M	W	H	J	N	L	A	O	S
C	E	R	E	G	I	O	N	F	V	Q
E	T	C	B	A	U	Z	A	R	I	I
F	K	I	M	P	O	R	T	A	N	T
P	E	V	A	L	U	J	I	S	C	N
K	R	I	B	H	G	D	O	L	E	T
Z	O	C	H	O	S	E	N	F	R	V

7. The word **parliament** comes from the French word **parler**, meaning **to speak**. A parliament is a place where people talk about certain problems. Some schools have parliaments where the teachers and students talk about problems.
   Write a speech that you might give if you were a member of your school's parliament.

20 OU as in Ouch!

country	fountain	favour	shoulder
labour	neighbour	course	wound
aloud	poured	surround	numerous
amount	though	surrounded	

1. Write
   (a) **sound** and all the words in the list that sound **ou** the same way.
   (b) the words in which **ou** has the sound of **u** in **fun**.
   (c) the word in which **ou** has a long **o** sound.
   (d) the words in which **ou** has the same sound as the **o** in **or**.
   (e) the word that has two different pronunciations.

2. (a) List in alphabetical order the two-syllable words that end in **our**. Many words that end in **our** may be spelled with **or**. Discuss with your teacher the preferred spelling in your area.
   (b) Write **poured** and underline its base word. Add **ing** to the base.
   (c) Divide **neighbour** and **labour** into syllables and then write the whole words. Underline the part in each word that gives the long **a** sound.

3. (a) Ask a question using the words **wound** and **shoulder**.
   (b) Make up two sentences for each of these words: **wound, favour, shoulder**. In one sentence use the word as a noun. In the other use it as a verb. Mark **N** over the word where it is a noun and **V** where you have used it as a verb.
   (c) Which word in the list is formed from **number**? Use the word in a sentence to show its meaning.

4. (a) Which words in the list are homonyms for **allowed** and **coarse**?
   (b) Which word rhymes with **mountain**?
   (c) What are the base words of **favourite** and **neighbourhood**?
   (d) Which words are formed from the base **round**?
   (e) Add the prefix **al** to **though**. Use your new word in a sentence.

5. Which Words Are These?
   (a) another name for work
   (b) something to cry on
   (c) someone you should love as yourself
   (d) not the city

6. Write two sentences to show two meanings of **country**.

7. Which words in the list contain these smaller words? First of all, use the clues below to get the smaller word. Then write the word from the list that contains the smaller word. For example,
   • short for laboratory   **lab   labour**
   • to name numbers in order
   • a big noise
   • climb
   • circular
   • sound a horse makes

8. Word Pictures
   Try some word pictures. Use the meaning of the word, or its sound, or some other idea the word gives you. Make the word into a picture. Some examples are given below. Other good words to use would be **fountain**, **country**, **poured**, and **shoulder**.

21 Prairie Roads

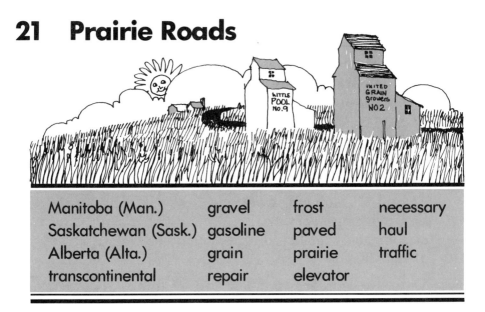

Manitoba (Man.)	gravel	frost	necessary
Saskatchewan (Sask.)	gasoline	paved	haul
Alberta (Alta.)	grain	prairie	traffic
transcontinental	repair	elevator	

1. (a) What three prairie provinces are named in the list?
        After each name give the abbreviation.
    (b) Which word in the list may be used to refer to wheat,
        oats, and barley?
    (c) What one name is given to the three provinces named
        in the list?

2. In your answers to these questions use the words in bold
    type. Use other words from the list if you can.
    (a) What vehicles are often used to **haul grain** to the
        elevator?
    (b) Why are the main highways in the **prairie** provinces
        paved?
    (c) Why is it often **necessary** to **repair** the roads in the
        spring?

3. (a) Look carefully at **necessary**. How many **c**'s has it?
        How many **s**'s has it? How many syllables has it?
        Write **necessary**. Circle the **c** and draw a line under
        the **ss**. What sound is made by the **c** and the **ss**?
    (b) Write **gravel** and **paved**. What is the sound of **a** in
        each word?
    (c) Which words in the list have double letters?
    (d) Which word in the list is a homonym of **hall**?

4. (a) Use **elevator** in a sentence to show a different meaning from the one in the picture.
   (b) List three other words that end in **or**. Use a dictionary if you need help.
   (c) Write **frost**. Tell two meanings of **frost** that are shown in these sentences.
      There was frost on the tree trunk.
      He is going to frost the cake.
   (d) Which word in the list means **across a continent**?
   (e) Write two other words that have the same prefix as the word you wrote in (d).

5. Some Riddles
   (a) Which word minus its prefix means two of something?
   (b) What province has a girl's name?
   (c) Which province has a sneeze in the middle of it?
   (d) What word is very wet without the protection of its first letter?

6. Name the province in which you would find each of these interesting place names. Use an atlas if you need help.
   (a) Flin Flon, (b) Medicine Hat, (c) Moose Jaw, (d) Portage la Prairie, (e) Viking, (f) North Battleford, (g) Wetaskiwin, (h) The Pas.

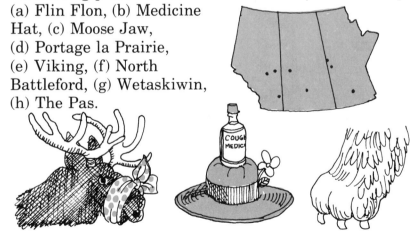

7. Prairie Fables
   A fable is an imaginary story that teaches a lesson or tells how something began. You may have read fables about how the tiger got its spots, or how the elephant got its trunk. Choose one of the places named in Exercise 6, and write a fable telling how the place got its name.

22 A Busy Pair

thought
right
neighbour
bought
brought
through
straight
delight
though
rough
tough
weigh
cough

bough
plough

The combination **gh** is one of the odd features of English spelling. How many different sounds for **gh** can you find in the words in the list?

1. Write
    (a) the words in which **gh** is not sounded.
    (b) the words in which these letters follow the long **i** sound.
    (c) the words in which **gh** follows **ei**; what sound does the combination **eigh** show? Write two other words you know that use this combination.
    (d) the word in which **aigh** shows a long **a** sound.

2. Make a chart on your page like the one below. Under each heading write the words in the list in which **ough** makes that sound.

ŭ (fun)	o͞o (blue)	ŏ (hot)	ō (hope)

3. (a) Make up two sentences in which you use **delight**. Use it as a noun in one sentence and as a verb in the other.
   (b) Add a suffix to **delight** and use the new word to describe something you bought.
   (c) Use **thought** as a noun and then as a verb in two different sentences.

4. (a) Add **er** and **est** to **rough** and then to **tough**.
   (b) Which words in the list are the opposites of **tender**, **smooth, crooked**?

5. (a) Write **neighbour**. Make new words by adding **ly** and **hood** to **neighbour**. Use each of your new words in a sentence.
   (b) Which words sound the same as **strait**, **way**, **ruff**, **threw**, **write**?
   (c) Write **though** and make a new word by adding the prefix **al**. Check in a dictionary to see if there is any difference in meaning between the two words.

6. Some Verse Is Worse Than Others
   Make up a few lines of verse to finish these. Then, if you wish, make up a whole verse of your own.
   • There was a young lady of eighty
     Who was far and away much too weighty.
     Though chocolates she bought not,
     As surely she ought not,

     . . . .

   • Tom Hough has had enough
     Of folks who say his name wrong.

     . . . .

23 Visiting the Atlantic Provinces

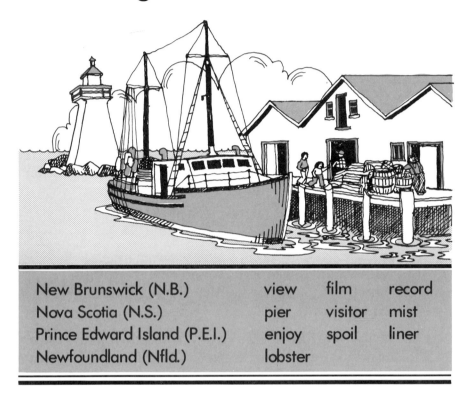

New Brunswick (N.B.)	view	film	record
Nova Scotia (N.S.)	pier	visitor	mist
Prince Edward Island (P.E.I.)	enjoy	spoil	liner
Newfoundland (Nfld.)	lobster		

1. Answer these questions, using one or more words from the list in each answer.
   (a) Name three of the Atlantic provinces and give the abbreviation for each one you name.
   (b) How do **visitors** keep a **record** of their trip to the Atlantic provinces?
   (c) Where is a good place to stand to get pictures of boats and ships?
   (d) What might spoil your view of the ocean on some days?
   (e) What is the famous food of the Atlantic provinces?

2. (a) Say **film** and **pier** carefully. How many syllables does each word have?
   (b) Write **film** and **pier**. Circle the sounded vowels.

3. Write
   (a) **visitor**; drop the suffix; make two new words by ad-

ding the suffix **ed**, then **ing** to the base word.

(b) **enjoy**; drop the prefix and write the new word; make another new word by adding the suffix **ment** to **enjoy**.

(c) **mist**; make a new word by adding the suffix **y**; write another word that sounds the same as **mist**.

(d) **view**; make another word by adding a prefix; add a different prefix and make another new word.

(e) two sentences to show two meanings of **liner**.

4. (a) Make up three questions in which you use **record**, **film**, and **view** as nouns.

(b) Now make up three statements in which you use **record**, **film**, and **view** as verbs.

(c) Which syllable is accented when **record** is a noun? Which is accented when **record** is a verb?

5. When writing the letters **b** and **v** you must be careful to join them correctly to the next letter. Unlike most letters, **b** and **v** are joined from the top.

(a) Write the three words in the list that contain the letter **v**. Join the letters carefully.

(b) Write the two words that contain the letter **b**.

6. (a) Which of the Atlantic provinces are islands?

(b) Which one is a peninsula?

(c) Name the Atlantic province in which you would find each of these places: Summerside, Annapolis, Grand Falls, Shippigan, Alberton, Glace Bay. Use an atlas if you need help.

7. Pretend that you work in a tourist office in one of the Atlantic provinces. Your job is to make people interested in coming to visit the area. Write a short paragraph for a travel folder, or make up three or four slogans to catch people's attention and make them want to come to the east coast.

24 Instant Replay

Many sports teams use instant replays to help them improve their performance. Replay these words to help you improve your understanding of them.

choose	necessary	neighbour	shoulder	though
province	region	parliament	nation	rural
important	poured	numerous	fountain	favour
prairie	elevator	traffic	repair	weigh
thought	tough	visitor	film	record

1. (a) List all the words that end in an **er** sound. Which two of these words contain a suffix?
   (b) Write all the words that contain the vowel pair **ou**.
   (c) Which three words in the list each contain two vowel pairs?

2. (a) Write all the one-syllable words in the list.
   (b) Which two words contain **ei** spelling a long **a** sound?
   (c) Which word contains two /s/ sounds? Circle the letters that make the /s/ sounds.

3. Which words could have these meanings?
   (a) a political division of Canada
   (b) the whole country
   (c) an area
   (d) a place where laws are discussed
   (e) many cars and trucks
   (f) outside the city

4. (a) One word in the list is contained in another word in the list. Write both words. How is the vowel sound different in the two words?
   (b) Write two sentences to show two uses and two pronunciations of **record**.
   (c) Which words were formed from these base words: **number, import, pour, elevate**?

5. The clues below are for small words or slang words that are contained in the words in the list. Write both the small word and the list word.
   (a) child's name for a train (same word twice)
   (b) ought to
   (c) a mischievous child

6. (a) Write the plurals of: **prairie, parliament, province, film**.
   (b) Add **ing** to **choose, pour, visit, record**.
   (c) Add **al** to **nation, region**; add **ial** to **province**.

7. Write **traffic** on your page as it is written below. Use the clues to find the words that begin with each letter in **traffic**. All the words except one are in the list. The missing one is in Unit 21.

   T 6/7 of **thought**
   R kind of area where most farms are
   A province and girl's name
   F fancy place to take a bath
   F act of kindness
   I what an education is
   C sounds like what he does with gum

1. (a) List the words that contain **gh**. After each word tell the sound that **gh** makes.
   (b) Put in alphabetical order the words that begin with **p** or **r**.

2. (a) In which two words are there three consonants together?
   (b) Add **ing** to **repair**, **film**, **weigh**.
   (c) Three words in the list begin and end with the same letters. Write the three words.

3. Which Word Am I?
   (a) Change my suffix to **al** and I stand for a number.
   (b) I record things in a camera.
   (c) I contain four vowels and five consonants, but only two syllables.
   (d) My middle is where ships come to dock.

4. Which words contain these smaller words or names? The spaces tell how many letters you must add.
   (a) P __ AIR __ __
   (b) __ __ __ VINCE
   (c) REG __ __ __
   (d) __ __ __ AL
   (e) T __ UG __
   (f) __ __ __ RED
   (g) __ H __ UG __ __

5. Word Square
   Use the clues to write the words that would fit in the square. The last word is not in the list.

Clues
1 Across: to fix
1 Down: to write down
2 Down: area
2 Across: fire-breathing monster

1. Write
   (a) **numerous** and three other words you know that end in **ous**.
   (b) **fountain** and three other words that end in **ain**.
   (c) **terrific** and three other words that end in **ic**.
   (d) **necessary** and two other words by adding the prefix **un** to make one word and the suffix **ity** to make the other.

2. (a) What is the base word of **elevator**? Add **ed** and **ing** to the base.
   (b) Change the first two letters of **shoulder** to one letter, to make a word that means a large rock.

   (c) The root of **repair** is the same as the root for **prepare**. Write two other words that are formed from the same root.

3. What is the difference
   (a) between a province and a region?
   (b) between a favour and a gift?
   (c) between a neighbour and a friend?

4. Tell the meaning of **favour** as it is used in these sentences. Use a dictionary if you need help.
   (a) I am in favour of building the bridge.
   (b) Do me a favour. Forget it.
   (c) He favoured his left leg.

5. Build the Towers
   Draw the towers on your page as they are drawn below. Be sure to put in the correct number of building blocks. Use the clues to help you build the towers.

   Clues (all the words except the last are in the list)
   1: where laws are made
   2 Down: what a broken bike needs
   2 Across: areas
   3 Down: part of the body minus **er**
   3 Across: what the windows did on a windy day

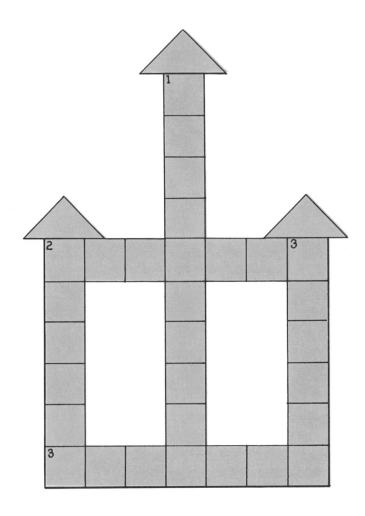

One Word — Two Uses

shock
patch
sting
force
search
grip
blame
knot
whip
whistle
waves
alarm
strap

Each word in this list may be used either as a noun or as a verb. **Patch** might be used as a noun like this: You need a patch on your jeans. **Patch** might be used as a verb like this: Did you patch your jeans yourself?

A frequent signal that a word is being used as a noun is that **a**, **an**, or **the** comes before it. Verb signals may be words such as **did** or **will**. Sometimes nouns and verbs do not have signals.

1. (a) Write **Noun** and **Verb** at the tops of two columns. Place in the correct columns the words in bold type in these sentences:

The rope was tied in a **knot**.
The horse will come if you **whistle**.
A good rider does not use a **whip**.
The pony had a white **patch** near its eye.
Did the bee **sting** your leg?
Make sure the **strap** is buckled tightly.

(b) For each noun in (a) write a sentence using the same word as a verb. For each verb, write a sentence using the same word as a noun.

(c) Use **waves** and **force** first as nouns and then as verbs.

2. Answer each question with a sentence using at least one word from the list.

(a) What time does the alarm clock ring in the morning at the ranch?

(b) When the alarm rings what do you force yourself to do?

(c) It is dark when you wake up. What do you search for?

3. (a) Which two words in the list rhyme?

(b) List in alphabetical order the words that end in silent **e**.

(c) Write the words that begin with two or more consonants.

(d) Which words have silent letters other than final **e**? Circle the silent letters.

4. (a) Write the words in the list that end in two or more consonants.

(b) Add **ed** and **ing** to each of the words you wrote in (a), except the word that does not have an **ed** form. What is the past tense of that word?

(c) Add **ed** and **ing** to the words that end in one consonant. What happens to the final consonant?

5. (a) Write the plural forms of the words that end in **ch**. How many syllables does the plural form of each word have?

(b) What change do you make in base words that end in **e** when you add **ed** or **ing**? Add these endings to the words that end in **e**.

6. Word Squares
   Make two squares on your page like the ones below. They
   are five spaces on each side. All the words except the last
   in each puzzle are in the list. Use the clues to fill in the
   words for each square.

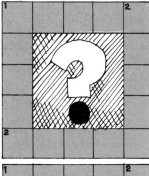

Clues
1. Across: holds the saddle on a horse
1. Down: what you get when you fall off a horse
2. Down: what you put on torn jeans
2. Across: a small sailing vessel

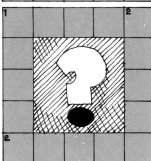

Clues
1. Across: what a flag does
1. Down: hits with a whip
2. Down: what bees do
2. Across: what you need if you have a broken arm

7. Life on the ranch is hard but it is interesting and healthful
   too. Write a story about a day's work on the ranch. Tell
   about some things you find hard and some things that you
   like to do.

Study the words in your personal spelling list.

26   Words That Describe

rapid	weak
cheap	famous
polite	holy
hollow	tame
silly	pure
swift	terrible
modern	terrific
damp	

tanned   clever

1. (a) Use a word from the list with each of the following nouns and its article. Use each word only once.

    the furniture   the grass   a motion
    a shrine   the cloth   a storm
    an invention   the muscles   a policeman

   (b) Look at your answers to (a) and tell where adjectives are often placed.

   (c) Write **swift** after the numbers of those animals which are swift runners.

   (d) Which word in the list means almost the same as **swift**?

2. Here are some other ways in which adjectives may be used. Write a word from the list that completes each sentence.
    (a) Our drinking water is _____ .
    (b) We met a _____ hockey player.
    (c) The skunk seems to be quite _____ .
    (d) The clown's actions were very _____ .
    (e) The automobile was invented in _____ times.

3. (a) Which two words in the list were formed from **terror**? Underline the double consonant in each.
   (b) How has the meaning of **terrific** changed from its former meaning, which was **to bring terror**?
   (c) The base word of one of the words in the list rhymes with another word in the list. Write the word, and then write its base and the other word that rhymes with it.

4. Write
   (a) two words in which **ea** represents the long **e** sound.
   (b) the words that end in **y**.
   (c) new words made by adding **er** and **est** to **holy**. How must you change the base word?
   (d) **modern** and two other words you know that end in **ern**.

5. **Swift**, **tame**, and **hollow** are usually adjectives, but they may be used as other parts of speech as well. Make up sentences in which you use them in these ways: **swift** as a noun, **tame** as a verb, **hollow** as a noun.

6. Can You Change Silly to Famous?
   • Write **silly**.
   • Drop one letter to get a word that means part of a window frame. Write the new word.
   • Change the first letter of the new word to get a word that means the opposite of **to empty**. Write the new word.
   • Change the vowel in the new word to get a word that means a season. Write that word.
   • Change the last two letters of the new word to get the base word of **famous**. Write the base word.
   • Add the correct suffix and you will have changed **silly** to **famous**.

7. Several of the words in the list may be used to describe various means of transportation. Write a short paragraph in which you tell the advantages and disadvantages of the most popular kinds of transportation in your area.

27 Back at the Ranch

offence

faithful	rodeo		
eagle	between	surprise	pleasant
hawk	jealous	beauty	loose
saddle	switch	toward	cement

1. Answer these questions using the words in bold type and other words from the list.
   (a) Why does a ranch hand need a **faithful** horse?
   (b) What might a rancher carry on his **saddle**?
   (c) What are two events at a **rodeo**?
   (d) How might a young calf give a ranch hand a **surprise**?

2. Which words
   (a) name birds?
   (b) are formed from **faith**? from **please**?
   (c) contain the same letter more than once?
   (d) do not have silent letters?

3. Noun and Verb
   One test for a noun is that it may follow one of the articles

a, **an**, or **the**. One test for a verb is that it may be used with **will** to refer to future time. Write two sentences for each of these words; use the word as a noun in one sentence and as a verb in the other: **saddle**, **switch**, **surprise**, **cement**.

4. Which words in the list could complete this sentence?
   He ran _____ the houses.
   The words that fit are **prepositions**.

5. Which words in the list could complete this sentence?
   She is a very _____ person.
   The words that fit are **adjectives**.

6. The clues below are for small words that are contained in words in the list. Write the small word and the list word for each clue.
   • small crawling insect
   • past form of **ride**
   • belief
   • not happy
   • broomstick rider

7. Bottom to Top
   The words in this puzzle must go from the bottom to the top. Draw the centre rectangle on your page. Then put in the correct number of spaces above and below it. Use the clues to find the words that fit, and discover the mystery word in the rectangle. All the answers are words in the list.

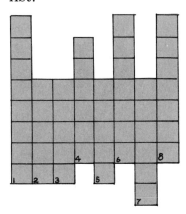

Clues
1. something not expected
2. large bird
3. riding and roping contest
4. good looks
5. not tight
6. filled with envy
7. what many sidewalks are made of
8. in the middle

28 Using Verbs

torn
instruct
allowed
failed
chosen
satisfied
spill
agree
greet
weigh
join
measure
studying
studied

deny
vanished
copy

All of these words may be used as verbs. Some may be used alone in a sentence; others need help. Some tell about the present time; others tell about the past. All verbs show time.

1. (a) Make two columns on your page. At the top of one, put the heading **Present**. At the top of the other, put the

heading **Past**. Place each of these verbs and their subjects in the Present column, and then fill in the Past column: **I tear, he fails, we agree, I greet, you study, they join, they float.**

(b) Write the form of these verbs that you would use with **have** or **has**: **choose, satisfy, tear, study, weigh.**

(c) For each of these words, write a word from the list that means the same: **teach, permitted, selected, overflow, contented.**

2. (a) Each of these words is a noun. Beside each write a verb in the list that is related to it: **satisfaction, choice, joint, greeting, student, agreement, instructor.**

(b) Make adjectives from these verbs by adding the suffix **able: agree, measure.** What happens to the final **e** in **measure** when you add the suffix?

3. Write
(a) two words that could mean **find the size of something.**

(b) another word you know in which **eigh** has the same sound that it has in **weigh.**

(c) **tear** twice; now write two other words, one to rhyme with each pronunciation that **tear** could have.

(d) the words that contain vowel pairs; circle the vowel that is sounded in each one except **weigh.** What is the vowel sound in **weigh**?

4. (a) Use **join** as a base word to make other words. First add the prefixes **ad** and **re** to the base and write the two new words. Then add the suffixes **ed** and **ing** to the base and write the two new words.

(b) Write a question in which you use **spill** as a verb.

(c) Now use **spill** as a noun in a statement.

5. Write
(a) the two words ending in **n** that need a helping verb in a sentence.

(b) **satisfied**; now write its base word.

(c) the words that are the opposite of **succeeded, forbade, unhappy.**

6. Tell how today's meaning of each word below is related to the original meaning. Use a dictionary if you need help, but use your own ideas too.

   (a) satisfied — from the Latin **satis** meaning **enough**

   (b) instruct — from the Latin **struere** meaning **to build**
   (c) weigh — from the Old English **wegan** meaning **to carry** or **to raise**
   (d) failed — from the Old French **faillir** meaning **to miss**

7. Build-a-Word
   In the sets of clues below, each clue gives you part of a word. When you have put the clues together in each set, you should have a word that is in the list.

   (a) short for Albert or Allan (b) short for Josephine
       opposite of **high**   opposite of **out**
       short for Edward

   (c) past form of **sit**   (d) plural personal pronoun
       I am; he __   three-quarters of **high**
       fried minus **r**

   (e) singular personal pronoun
       __ clear __ glass (same word)
       last half of **future**

Adverbs: What They Look Like and What They Do

1
densely
extremely
certainly
kindly
immediately
properly

2
main
jealous
excellent
faithful

3
nowhere
farther
further
backwards
forward

Many adverbs end in **ly**. Many adverbs tell **how**, **when**, or **where**.

1. (a) Write the words in the first column.
    (b) Draw a circle around the letters that are the same in every word.
    (c) Write the base word for each word in the first column. Each of these base words is an adjective.
    (d) Tell one way in which an adjective may be made into an adverb.

2. (a) Write each word in the second column.
   (b) Add **ly** to each word you wrote in (a).
   (c) How have you changed the part of speech by adding **ly**?
   (d) The last three words in Column 2 can be made into nouns also. Add a suffix to each of these to make it a noun.

3. (a) Which two words contain the suffix **ward** or **wards**?
   (b) Write again the word you wrote in (a) that could be either an adjective or an adverb. How is the word you just wrote different in spelling from the other word?
   (c) How are the two words you wrote in (a) related in meaning?
   (d) Write two other words you know that have the suffix **ward**.
   (e) Which word in the list is a compound word?
   (f) Write two other compound words you know in which the second part is **where**.

4. Write
   (a) the word in the list that means **at once**.
   (b) the words in the list that could mean the same as **thickly**, **surely**, **very**, **correctly**.
   (c) a word that describes a dog that is true to its master.

   (d) a word that tells how warm it might be at the equator.
   (e) a name often given to the most important street in a town.
   (f) a person who doesn't want people to pay any attention to anyone else.

5. (a) Which of these questions is answered by each word in Column 1: **how? when? where?**
   (b) Which of those three questions could be answered by the first three words in Column 3?
   (c) Write three adverbs you know that answer the question **when**.

6. The words **further** and **farther** are very close in meaning but are not quite the same. Different dictionaries define them in different ways. Look up each word in at least two dictionaries, and then write each word in a sentence that makes its meaning clear. Read your sentences to at least one of your classmates and have classmates read theirs to you. Discuss the meanings that each of you has.

7. Swifties
   Here are two "Swifties":
   "Give me the **knife**," he said **cuttingly**.
   "There is **no wind**," the sailor said **calmly**.
   To make a Swiftie, think of a short sentence containing a word to which you can relate an adverb, as **knife-cuttingly**, and **no wind-calmly** are related. Put your sentence into a quotation and make your adverb describe the speaker.
   "Is supper ready?" she asked hungrily.
   Make up three or four Swifties and share them with your friends.

30 Making Sure

beauty	modern	satisfied	kindly
studying	allowed	extremely	immediately
famous	nowhere	excellent	cheap
between	chosen	force	jealous
instruct	search		agree
certainly	terrible		shock
whistle	saddle		measure

1. (a) Write in alphabetical order the three words in the list that would be closest to the front of a dictionary and the three words that would be closest to the back.
   (b) Which words in the list end in **ly**? What part of speech is each of these words?
   (c) What is the base word of each word you wrote in (b)?

2. (a) Which words in the list would complete this sentence? What part of speech is each word that fits?
   That is a _____ building.
   (b) Which words would complete this sentence? What part of speech is each of the words that fit?
   He will _____ the group.

3. (a) Which words were formed from these base words: **choose, excel, satisfy, where, fame**?
   (b) Write the words in the list that contain the **ea** vowel pair. After each word write the sound the **ea** vowel pair makes.
   (c) Write **saddle**. Change the first letter to **p** and write the new word. Now change the second letter of the new word to **u**. What is the new word?
   (d) Which word is a compound? Make new words by changing the first part to **some, any, else**.

4. (a) Which words are the opposites of **unknown, old-fashioned, ease, expensive, forbidden**?
   (b) Which words in the list are the base words of these: **jealousy, shocking, whistling, agreeable, beautiful**?

5. A rich lady died and left her estate to be divided **between** her husband and her seven children. The lawyer for the children argued that the will should say **among** the husband and seven children. Explain what difference it would make to use **among** instead of **between**.

6. Write each word below. Then change the suffix to the one in brackets and write the new words.
   * satisfied (action)
   * studying (ent)
   * allowed (able)
   * terrible (ify)

7. Famous Word Search
   Ten words from the list are in the puzzle below. You can see one easily. Find and write the other nine.

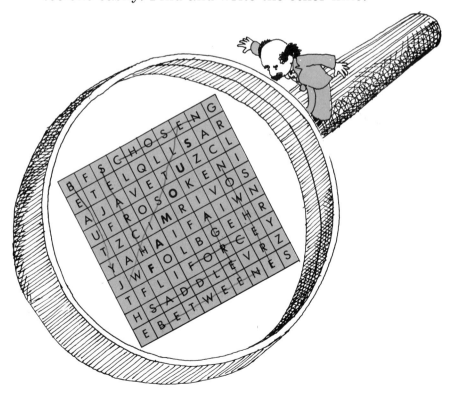

1. (a) Which words in the list contain double consonants?
   (b) Which words contain double vowels?
   (c) In which words is **c** the second last letter?

2. Well, Well!
   Which words could have these meanings?
   - well known
   - well done
   - well pleased
   - well, sure
   - well priced
   - well intentioned

3. (a) Which three words have three **e**'s?
   (b) Which five words have two **e**'s?
   (c) Which six words have **y** spelling the long **e** sound?

4. (a) Which words contain these smaller words?
      am low now sat cell sure
   (b) Which words mean the same or nearly the same as these?
      teach look for content awful picked

5. (a) Add **ing** to **whistle, measure, force, saddle**. How must you change the base word before adding **ing**?
   (b) Write the plurals of **whistle, search, force, saddle, shock**.

6. Write **satisfied** as it is written below, and include the dashes and circles. Use the clues to find the words that fit. Then unscramble the circled letters to answer the second part of the puzzle. All the words but one are in the list.

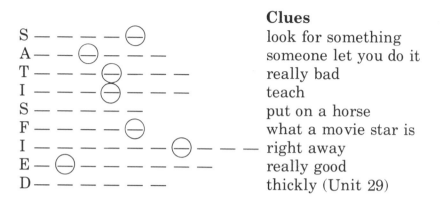

Clues

S — — — — ⊖	look for something
A — — ⊖ — — —	someone let you do it
T — — — ⊖ — — —	really bad
I — — — ⊖ — — —	teach
S — — — — — —	put on a horse
F — — — — ⊖	what a movie star is
I — — — — — — — ⊖ — — —	right away
E — ⊖ — — — — — — —	really good
D — — — — — — —	thickly (Unit 29)

Unscramble the circled letters to find the name of a bird with long legs and a long neck.

For Good Spellers

1. Explain the meaning of these sayings.
   (a) Beauty is only skin deep.
   (b) Measure unto others as it is measured unto you.
   (c) We were caught between the devil and the deep blue sea.

2. (a) Write **extremely**, its base, and three other words that begin with **extr**.
   (b) List four other words that begin with **mod**.

3. Roots
   (a) Write **immediately**. Find its root by dropping the prefix and two suffixes. List three other words formed from the same root.
   (b) The root of **kindly** is **kin** which is also the root of **king**. Give three other words formed from the same root.
   (c) The root of **certainly** is **cert** (from **certus**). Write three other words from that root.
   (d) The root of **instruct** is **stru** (from **struere**, to build). Give three other words from the same root.

4. Add prefixes or suffixes as necessary to words in the list or their bases to find words that complete the sentences.
   (a) If a goal is scored, but it does not count, it is _____ .
   (b) A person who is well known for bad deeds is _____ .
   (c) If a person will never agree, he is _____ .
   (d) A person who is not sure is _____ .
   (e) An achievement that has never been done better is

   _____ .

5. What's Your Word I.Q.?
   The definitions below are for words that are contained in words in the list. Write the small word and the list word. Here is how to score:
   • all right without using a dictionary — **Genius**
   • all right using a dictionary — **Very Bright**
   • three or four right without a dictionary — **Bright**
   • three or four right with a dictionary — **Smart**
   • less than three or four right — **You're still no dummy!**
   (a) a wager
   (b) one's family or relatives
   (c) to burn or dry up
   (d) a card game something like bridge
   (e) boy friend (French word)

union	who's
manual	proof
truth	lose
huge	broom
fuel	smooth
whose	prove
	moose
utensil	secure

There are two sounds that are called **long u**. One of these sounds is the same as the word **you**. It is in the words **use** and **cube**. Dictionaries usually mark this sound ū. The other sound is in words like **loose** and **move**. Dictionaries usually mark this sound o͞o or o͝o. This second sound has many different spellings.

1. (a) Make two columns on your paper under the headings ū and o͞o. Under each heading, write the words in the list that have that sound.
   (b) In the o͞o column, mark the letters that make this sound in each word.

2. (a) Write **whose** and its base word.
   (b) Which other word in the list is formed from the same base?
   (c) Write the two words for which the word you wrote in (b) is a contraction.
   (d) Write the word that would correctly complete each sentence below.

   _____ that boy standing beside the school?
   _____ books are these on the shelf?

3. (a) Write four words from the list that contain **oo**.
    (b) Add **ly** to one of these words and write the new word.
    (c) Write sentences to show the two meanings of **proof** in these sentences.
        You should **proofread** all your work.
        Show me the **proof** for your answer to the math question.
    (d) **Proof** is a noun. Write the word in the list that is the verb that corresponds to it.

4. (a) Write **fuel** and **huge**. After each write the number of syllables it has.
    (b) Now write the same two words again. Circle the last two letters of each and notice how they differ in spelling and in sound.

5. Make these sentences mean the opposite by changing the word in bold type to a word from the list.
    (a) Did you **find** your mother's driving manual?
    (b) The ice on the river was **rough** and thick.
    (c) We flew in a **small** airplane.

6. (a) Answer these questions using **manual** instead of the words in bold type.
        Does the car have **hand** controls?
        Do you have a **handbook** that tells what fuel to use?
    (b) Write **manual**. Make a new word by adding **ly** to it. Use the new word in a sentence to show that you know its meaning.

7. What Am I?
    (a) When I am new I sweep clean.
    (b) In court, people tell all of me and nothing but me.
    (c) My root word is related to **onion** and **pearl**.

8. Each underlined word in the story below is a small word that is contained in one of the words in the list. Write the words from the list.
    Ruth crawled out of her **room** onto the **roof**. A **man** watering his lawn with a **hose** got her down. She gave him a big **hug**.

Cast Ashore

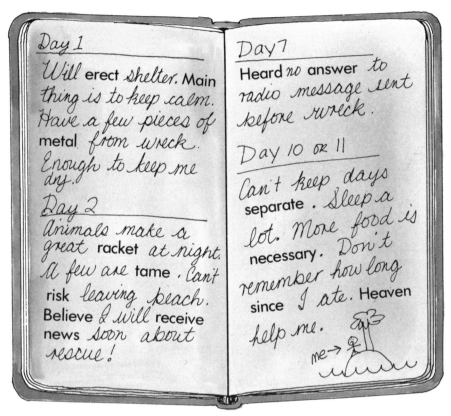

32

Day 1

Will erect shelter. Main thing is to keep calm. Have a few pieces of metal from wreck. Enough to keep me dry.

Day 2

Animals make a great racket at night. A few are tame. Can't risk leaving beach. Believe I will receive news soon about rescue!

Day 7

Heard no answer to radio message sent before wreck.

Day 10 or 11

Can't keep days separate. Sleep a lot. More food is necessary. Don't remember how long since I ate. Heaven help me.

me →

The words for study in this unit are the ones in bold type in the story.

1. Use the words in bold type and others from the story in your answers to these questions.
   (a) From what will the person **erect** a shelter?
   (b) What did the person **believe**?
   (c) Why do you think the person could not keep the days **separate**?

2. Make a chart on your page like the one below. Under each heading write the study words from the story that belong.

Long **e** (sleep)	Short **e** (get)	e+/r/ (gear)	Silent **e**

3. Write
   (a) **receive** and **believe**. What sound of **e** do both words contain? How are the letters that stand for the sounds different in each word?
   (b) **separate**. What two vowels are each used twice in this word? Write two sentences to show two uses and two pronunciations of **separate**.
   (c) **necessary**. How many syllables are in this word? **Necessary** is often misspelled because one of the syllables is not carefully pronounced.
   (d) Drop the **ary** from **necessary** and change the first letter to **r**. What is the new word?
   (e) **news**. What other study word in the story has the four letters of **news** in it?

4. (a) Add **ing** to these words: **erect, risk, answer**.
   (b) Add **ing** to **tame, receive, separate, believe**.
   (c) How did you change the base word before adding the endings in (b)?

5. Look at the words in bold type in these sentences. For each word tell its meaning as it is used in the story and also its meaning in the sentence below. Use a dictionary for help.
   (a) The soldier stood **erect**.
   (b) She has a new tennis **racket**.
   (c) There was a broken water **main** on our street.

6. What's the Difference?
   (a) between **erect** and **build**
   (b) between **necessary** and **wanted**
   (c) between **separate** and **join**
   (d) between **tame** and **friendly**
   (e) between **heard** and **listened**

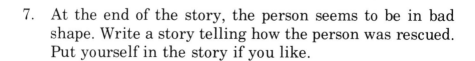

7. At the end of the story, the person seems to be in bad shape. Write a story telling how the person was rescued. Put yourself in the story if you like.

33

Some Ways To Spell Long e

cheek	cheat	keen	treat
screen	machine	study	steering
freedom	machinery	taxi	complete
key	sweep		

alley	keel	grease

1. (a) Make two columns on your page. At the top of one put the heading **ee**. At the top of the other put the heading **ea**. Under each heading write the words in the list that use that spelling for the long **e** sound.
   (b) Three other ways of spelling the long **e** sound appear in the list. Make three groups of words to show these other ways.

2. Making New Words
   Make as many new words as you can for each item below:
   (a) replace the final consonant of **keen**.
   (b) add suffixes to **screen**, **study**, **sweep**.
   (c) add prefixes and suffixes to **complete**.

3. Write
   (a) the base words of **freedom** and **steering**.
   (b) three other words that end in **dom**.
   (c) two sentences to show two meanings of **steer**.
   (d) the words in the list that contain **ch**. Underline **ch** in the words in which it makes the /sh/ sound.

4. Complete the Sayings
   Use words from the list to complete these common sayings.
   (a) Turn the other _____ .
   (b) New brooms _____ clean.
   (c) Hard work is the _____ to success.
   (d) Every citizen has a right to _____ of speech.

5. You Be the Dictionary
   Write short meanings for the words in bold type in these sentences.
   (a) We watched the movies on the **screen**.
       Our door has a **screen** in it.
   (b) She is a very **keen** student.
       The knife has a **keen** edge.
   (c) We had a **treat** for dessert.
       The doctor will **treat** the patient.
   (d) We went to the airport in a **taxi**.
       Soon the huge plane will **taxi** down the runway.

6. It Could Be Verse
   Complete the following verses either as limericks or as little jingles. Or, if you wish, write your own verse instead.
   • There once was a fellow so keen,
     He invented a strange new machine.

   • What shall I tell my dear old buddy?
     He wants to play when I have to study.

94

Doctor's Work

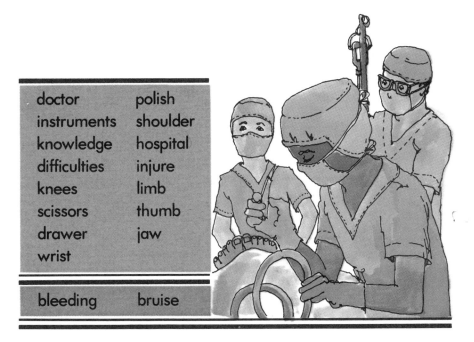

doctor	polish
instruments	shoulder
knowledge	hospital
difficulties	injure
knees	limb
scissors	thumb
drawer	jaw
wrist	
bleeding	bruise

1. Which words
   (a) name parts of the body?
   (b) name things a doctor uses?

2. Write
   (a) the words in the list that are formed from **know**, **difficult**, **draw**.
   (b) the word that tells where a doctor sometimes works.
   (c) the four plural nouns.
   (d) a word that could mean an arm or a leg or a part of a tree.
   (e) **hospital**: add the suffix **ity** and use the new word in a sentence to show that you know what it means.

3. (a) Three words in the list begin with silent letters. Write the words and circle the silent letters.
   (b) Write the three words that end in silent consonants and circle the silent letters.
   (c) What vowel is silent in **shoulder**? Write the word and underline the silent vowel.

(d) **Scissors** is an unusual word in meaning and in sound. It has no singular. Write **scissors**. Underline the letters that make the /z/ sound in two different places in the word.

4. (a) Write **polish**. What sound does the vowel have? Now write the same word with a capital letter. What sound does the vowel have in the capitalized word? What does this word mean?

(b) Write **injure**. Is it a noun or a verb? Now make a new word by adding **y**. What change must you make in the base word? Is the new word a noun or a verb?

(c) Which word in the list ends in **or**? Write that word and two other words you know that end in **or**.

(d) Write the word in the list that ends in **al** and two other words you know that end the same way.

5. Mini-Riddles
The answers to these riddles are smaller words that are contained in words in the list. Write the small word and the word from the list.
(a) I can make a picture.
(b) I am what you do with a guitar.
(c) I am a narrow shelf near a window, or a ridge of rock.
(d) I mean the same as **knots** or I can be articles of men's clothing.

6. A doctor's work is interesting but also difficult. Write a paragraph in which you tell why you might like to be a doctor or why you would not like to be a doctor when you are an adult.

LARGE PROPERTY FOR SALE OR RENT
Half-timber dwelling, two storeys and finished attic. Car shelter at rear. At edge of
densely-wooded ravine. General improve-
ment loan available. Consider any price
offered. Reply P.O. Box 479.

property	densely	shelter	general
offered	rent	loan	timber
fortune	edge	worth	borrow
attic	receipt	rotten	

	average	lodge

1. Answer the questions below using information from the advertisement. Use at least one word from the list in each answer.
   (a) Of what material is the house built?
   (b) Where is the house located?
   (c) What is the third storey like?
   (d) Where is the car shelter?
   (e) How could a person get money for the improvements that are needed?

2. (a) Write the words in the list that are used in the advertisement.
   (b) Which words are not in the advertisement?
   (c) Write a short answer to the advertisement, in which you offer to rent the house.

3. Tell the meaning of **general** as it is used in each sentence below.
   He is a general in the army.
   The village has a general store.
   There is a general interest in hockey.

4. Write
   (a) **densely** and another word that could replace it in the advertisement.
   (b) **worth** and a sentence that tells how much the property is worth.
   (c) **fortune** and two sentences to show two meanings of the word.
   (d) **receipt** and another word that starts the same and means **to get** or **to take in**.
   (e) **loan** and **borrow** and tell how they are related in meaning.

5. (a) List all the words that have double letters. Box the double letters in each word.
   (b) What are the base words of **offered**, **densely**, **rotten**?
   (c) Write **edge**. Make three new words by adding one or more letters to the beginning of **edge**.

6. (a) The word **property** is related to the word **proper**. Tell

how you think the meanings of the words are related.
(Hint: Think about proper names.)

(b) What do you call a person who **borrows**?
What do you call a person who **loans**?

(c) What might cause the **timber** in a house to become **rotten**?

7. Write an advertisement offering a fine piece of timberland for sale or rent. Suggest some advantages of your property. For example, how might it be used?

8. Names in Words
Below are some names that can be found in the words in the list. The blanks show how many letters you must add to make the words. Write the whole word that contains each name.

(a) __ __ __ __ __ AL
(b) T I M __ __ __
(c) R O __ __ __ N
(d) __ __ F __ R E D
(e) E D __ __

36 Time for a Spring Tune-up

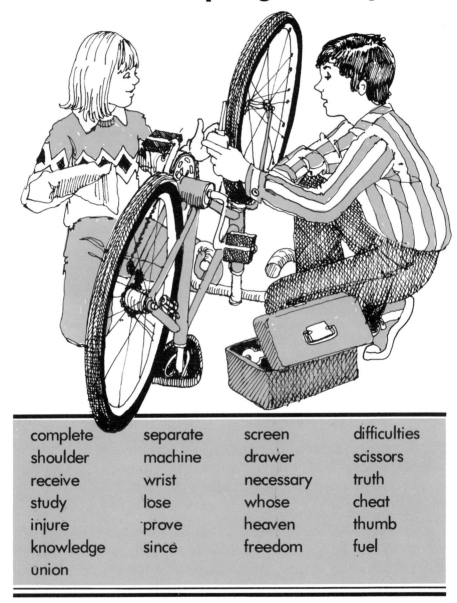

complete	separate	screen	difficulties
shoulder	machine	drawer	scissors
receive	wrist	necessary	truth
study	lose	whose	cheat
injure	prove	heaven	thumb
knowledge	since	freedom	fuel
union			

Many machines need a spring tune-up to put them in the best working order. Your spelling machine may need a tune-up too. These questions should help.

1. (a) Which words in the list are related to these words: **proof**, **true**, **free**, **lost**, **draw**?
   (b) Add **ing** to these words: **study**, **complete**, **receive**, **lose**, **prove**. How must you change the last four base words before adding **ing**?
   (c) Which words contain the **ea** vowel pair? After each word, tell the sound the **ea** makes.
   (d) Two words have silent consonants at the beginning, and one has a silent consonant at the end. Write the three words and circle the silent consonants.

2. (a) Which words in the list are plural in form?
   (b) Which of the words you wrote in (a) has no singular form?
   (c) What is the singular form of the other word you wrote in (a)?
   (d) Give the plural form of each of these words: **shoulder**, **machine**, **screen**, **drawer**, **union**.

3. Word Patterns
   Let **C** stand for any consonant and **V** stand for any vowel. Which words fit these patterns?
   - C-V-C-V
   - C-C-V-C-C
   - C-V-C-V-C-V-C-V
   - C-V-V-C
   - C-V-C-C-V

4. (a) Which words contain the /z/ sound? Circle the letter or letters that make the sound in each word.
   (b) In which words does the letter **c** stand for the /s/ sound?

5. Which words could have these meanings?
   - something known
   - to hurt
   - needed
   - to set apart
   - finished

6. (a) Arrange in alphabetical order all the words in the list that begin with the letter **s**.
   (b) Write **drawer**. It looks as though **drawer** should mean **one who draws** or **a thing which draws**. Explain the meaning of **drawer** as it might be used in art and as a part of a cabinet.

7. You've Created a Monster!
   Sketch the outline of a monster like the one below. Be sure to allow the correct number of spaces in each part. Use the clues to fill in the parts. All the words except 4 Down are in the list.

Clues

1: what mechanics work on (plural)
2 Across: the gravelled side of a road
2 Down: what movies are shown on
3 Down: where God is said to be
4 Down: most cars have this in front; a few have it in the back
5 Down: what you like to do with mail
6 Down: what you must have to build a monster
7 Down: what a few spare parts are

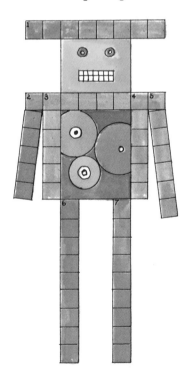

Remember the study steps (p. 5)!

1. Which words
   (a) have either a double vowel or a double consonant?
   (b) contain the letter **w**? What sound does the letter **w** make in each word? (Be careful.)
   (c) begin or end with two consonants making one sound?
   (d) name parts of the body?

2. (a) Write the words that are the opposites of: **find**, **lie**, **slavery**, **useless**, **join**, **give**.
   (b) Which words contain these smaller words: **heat**, **hum**, **par**, **know**, **sin**?

3. Which words could have these meanings?
   (a) something that can be burned to make a fire
   (b) instrument for cutting
   (c) object that does work for people
   (d) a cover for protection
   (e) a group of people

4. Which Word Am I?
   (a) Change my last letter to a suffix and I am what you are.
   (b) Add **rely** and I mean almost the same as **truly**.
   (c) Change my first letter and I might make you cry.
   (d) Change my last letter to **y** and I hope you never have me.
   (e) Add an **s** and I mean the sky above.

5. Mystery Word

Draw a rectangle on your page like the one below. Be sure to allow the correct number of spaces above and below the rectangle. Use the clues to fill in the spaces with words from the list. To get 7 Down, you will have to know the word for the rectangle.

Clues

1. hardships
2. keeps bugs out
3. opposite of give
4. do something dishonestly
5. prepare for test
6. what every team does sometimes
7. found in large factory

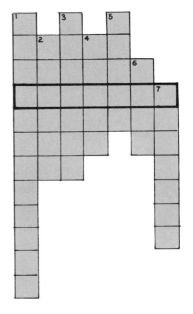

For Good Spellers

1. Write
   (a) **fuel** and name five kinds of fuel.
   (b) **scissors** and five other cutting instruments.
   (c) **thumb** and three other words that end in **mb**.
   (d) **machine** and three other words that have the letters **ch** making the /sh/ sound.

2. (a) Using a different vowel or vowel combination each time, write as many rhyming words for **lose** as you can.

(b) What is the **tion** form of **receive**? The root of the new word is **cept**. Write three other words from the same root.

3. Big Words for Common Sayings
The sayings below use big words; the usual forms of the sayings are much simpler. Write the simple form of each. One word from each saying is in the list.
   (a) It is more beneficial to render than it is to be rendered unto.
   (b) Apply that part of your anatomy to which your upper limbs are attached to the circular object.
   (c) He is increasing the quantity of combustible material in the conflagration.

4. Body Oddities
The words in each pair below are related in their origins. Tell how you think each pair is related in meaning.
   • **wrist** and **write**
   • **thumb** and **tumour**
   • **shoulder** and **shield**

5. What's That Coming Through the Screen?
Write **screen** as it is below, being sure to allow the correct number of spaces. Use the clues to fill in the spaces. Then unscramble the circled letters and add them to the hint below to find out what is coming through the screen.

Clues
   • used for cutting
   • may contain a motor
   • split apart
   • be given
   • worth fighting for
   • starts with **sin**

   ◯ — — S — ◯ — —
   ◯ — C — — — ◯
   — — — — R — ◯ —
   — — — E ◯ — —
   — — — E — ◯ —
   ◯ — N — —

Answer
   — — — Q U — — — — —

37 Gardening

orchard
shower
hose
prevent
mower
drain
sprinkle
chopped

spade
ladder
control
irrigation
spruce

daisy
branch

Today **orchard** means an area where fruit trees are grown. Long ago **orchard** was a compound word that meant **garden-yard**. The old word was spelled **ortgeard**. If you say the **g** with a /j/ sound, you can see how the word came to have its present spelling. **Ort** is from a Latin word **hortus**, meaning **garden**, and **geard** is the old spelling of **yard**.

1. Write
   (a) **orchard**; after it write five words from the list that refer to ways of providing water for an orchard.
   (b) the name of a machine that cuts grass in the orchard.
   (c) a sentence in which you use **control** and the word you wrote in (b).

2. Describe in a sentence or two how you would use a **spade** and a **ladder** in an orchard.

3. Use the words in bold type in your answers to these questions.
   (a) Why might an orchard need **irrigation**?
   (b) When would you have to **drain** land?
   (c) What might you **sprinkle** on the leaves of trees?
   (d) Why is a spring **shower** often welcome?

   (e) What could spraying **prevent**?
   (f) Why might a line of **spruce** trees be put along one side of an orchard?

4. (a) Make up two sentences to show two different meanings of **hose**.
   (b) What is the base word of **irrigation**?
   (c) Write **prevent**; add **ion** and write the new word.

5. Write
   (a) **shower** and **mower**; how is the **ow** sound different in each? Write two other words that have the same **ow** sound as each of these.
   (b) **chopped** and its base word.
   (c) **control**; make new words by adding **ed** and **ing**.

6. Riddles
   (a) Chop the ending off me and you have a young boy.
   (b) Some people think it is unlucky to walk under me.
   (c) Take away my first two letters and my last two letters and you will have, a place to skate.

7. Write **orchard** as it is written below. Use each letter as the first letter in a word that names a tree, a fruit, or a vegetable. One is done for you (an easy one).

   O
   R
   C
   H
   A P P L E
   R
   D

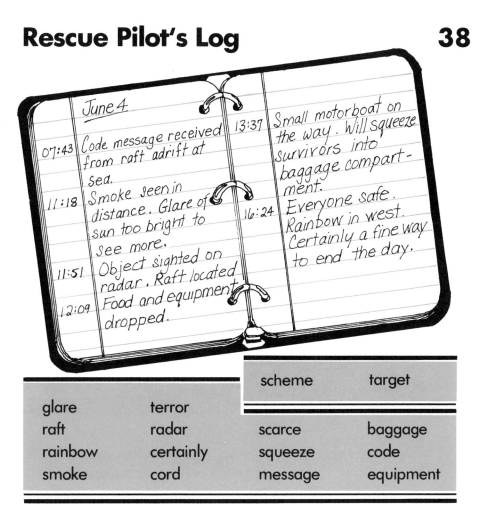

June 4

07:43 Code message received from raft adrift at sea.

11:18 Smoke seen in distance. Glare of sun too bright to see more.

11:51 Object sighted on radar. Raft located.

12:09 Food and equipment dropped.

13:37 Small motorboat on the way. Will squeeze survivors into baggage compartment.

16:24 Everyone safe. Rainbow in west. Certainly a fine way to end the day.

		scheme	target
glare	terror		
raft	radar	scarce	baggage
rainbow	certainly	squeeze	code
smoke	cord	message	equipment

1. Answer these questions using information from the story.
   (a) What happened at 07:43?
   (b) What was the first sign of the raft that the pilot saw?
   (c) What was dropped from the plane?
   (d) Where were the survivors put on the motorboat?
   (e) What two things made a fine end to the day?

2. Use words from the list that are **not** in the story to answer these questions.
   (a) What might the people on the raft have felt?
   (b) What might have been used to hold the parts of the raft together?
   (c) What might have been **scarce** on the raft?

3. Which word ... ?
   - is spelled the same forward and backward
   - contains three **r**'s • contains three **e**'s
   - contains three **g**'s • is a compound word

4. Write
   (a) two words in the list that are not in their base form.
   (b) the base form of each word you wrote in (a).
   (c) **terror** and two other words formed from **terror**.

5. Which words in the list have these meanings?
   (a) very strong shining light
   (b) great fear
   (c) secret writing
   (d) not plentiful
   (e) trunks, suitcases, etc., that a traveller carries

6. Build the Raft
   The words that fit in the logs of the raft are all in the list.
   Use the clues below to write on your own paper the words
   that fit. When you have done them all you will have built
   the raft.

   Clues
   1. the log on each side
      has a suffix
   2. one log starts with
      a very untidy word
   3. one log starts with
      a wet word
   4. one log ends like
      sneeze
   5. one log starts with
      a small paper or
      plastic container

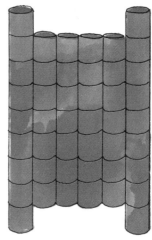

ENGAGEMENT ANNOUNCED

UPPEN - DOWNE

Victoria, May 24. - At a brief ceremony, held on the lawn of the Uppen home, the engagement of Ursula Uppen and Dwayne Downe was announced. The Uppen-Downe wedding will take place on Sept. 10. Following the announcement, neighbours and members of the press enjoyed a lunch of sandwiches and other items. Later, the guests were introduced to Reverend Smiley who will unite the couple in marriage. Reverend Smiley is a cousin of the future husband.

Ursula Uppen

Dwayne Downe

wrapped	unite	neighbour	sandwiches
press	items	introduced	hymn
wedding	delight	engagement	husband
lawn	wife	wives	

blessing	jewellery

1. Answer these questions using the words in bold type. Try to use other words from the list also.
   (a) Where was the **engagement** ceremony held?
   (b) What are the names of the future **husband** and **wife**?
   (c) What other **items** might have been included in the lunch?
   (d) Why was Reverend Smiley **introduced** to the group?

2. (a) Which words in the list were not used in the announcement?
   (b) Use these words in one or two sentences describing the wedding.

3. (a) Write **introduced**. Drop the prefix and the ending, and circle the root of this word. Make new words by adding the prefixes **pro** and **re** to the root.
   (b) Write **introduced** again. This time, change the ending to **ing**. How must you change the base word?

4. (a) One word has both singular and plural forms in the list. Write both forms.
   (b) Which words were formed from these bases: **engage**, **wrap**, **sandwich**, **wed**, **item**?
   (c) In which words do you hear the short **i** sound?
   (d) Which of the words you wrote in (c) does not contain the letter **i**?

5. Other Meanings of Common Words
   Use a dictionary to help you with this exercise.
   (a) **Press** may refer to newspapers. Find two other meanings of **press**, and write a sentence to show each meaning.
   (b) Find another meaning of **husband**, and write a sentence to show this meaning.

6. **Unite** means **to make one**. Use these clues to write other words that have something to do with **one**. Each word starts with **uni**.
   (a) clothes worn by police officers or soldiers
   (b) singing as with one voice (The group sang in _____ .)
   (c) a group of people joined together for some purpose

7. Write the word **delight** as it is written here, being sure to use the correct number of spaces. You will need eleven spaces going down. Use the clues to fill in the spaces. Then unscramble the circled letters to find out who three surprise guests at the wedding were.

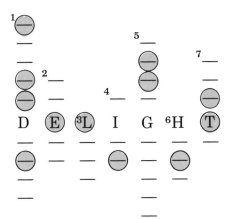

Clues

1. made known to
2. things or articles
3. grassy area
4. married woman
5. promise to marry
6. song of praise
7. put together

Who were the three surprise guests? Use **L** twice. (Hint: The three guests escaped from a nearby zoo. One of them has a four-letter name; the others have five-letter names.)

Remember to keep and to use your personal spelling list.

40　The Last Roundup

Just before you leave this book, let's have one more roundup of
your skills with some of the trickiest words.

certainly	necessary	introduced	prairie
acquainted	imagine	pattern	sandwiches
immediately	measure	prevent	losing
though	neighbour	complete	choose
dictionary	league	flashlight	lawn
control	practice	knees	surround
beauty			

1.　(a)　Which words in the list are not in their base forms?
　　(b)　Write the base form of each word you wrote in (a).
　　(c)　Which words in the list would be found in a dictionary
　　　　between the words **make** and **prince**?

2.　Make New Words
　　Write each of these words. Beside each write the form of
　　the word using the suffix shown in brackets. Be sure to
　　change the base word when you need to.
　　(a)　beauty　(ful)　　　　　(d)　surround　(ings)
　　(b)　imagine　(ation)　　　(e)　control　(ed)
　　(c)　complete　(ion)

3. (a) Which words in the list are plural?
   (b) Write the singular form of each word you wrote in (a).
   (c) Give the plural form of **dictionary**, **practice**, **league**, **prairie**, **pattern**.

4. Small and Large
   The clues below are for small words that can be found in words in the list. Write both the small word and the list word that contains it.
   (a) a rule made by a government
   (b) circular, not square
   (c) sudden burst of light
   (d) sound a horse makes
   (e) tiny grains of rock

5. Some Cutting Questions
   The clues below are not definitions, but they each suggest a word in the list. Which words do you think they refer to?
   (a) what you do before you cut
   (b) what you might cut many times this summer
   (c) what you might cut if you fall down
   (d) what you might cut with a knife before putting them into a picnic basket
   (e) what you might cut if you are getting ready to make something

6. Which word in the list could you use to tell a person
   (a) where to find the meaning of a word?
   (b) that you know someone?
   (c) that you have finished?
   (d) that you can keep something from happening?
   (e) that you live on a large flat area of land with few trees?

7. Double Puzzle
   Draw a rectangle on your page like this one, being sure to put the correct number of spaces above and below. Use the clues to find the words that fill the spaces. When you have done that correctly, you will know the mystery word. All the words except number 9 are in the list.
   Unscramble the circled letters to find what we wish you a whole lot of for the summer.

Clues

1. joints in the legs
2. good looks
3. what you need in order to do better
4. a group of teams
5. helpful at night
6. behind in a contest
7. east of the Rocky Mountains, west of Ontario
8. what attackers do to a fort
9. what you can do with chicken, eggs, or fish

Extra Help

1. Which words
   (a) contain six letters but only one syllable?
   (b) contain more than three syllables?
   (c) have silent consonants? (Do not count double letters.)

2. (a) Write the word in the list that ends in **ing**.
   (b) Give the **ing** form of **prevent**, **imagine**, **measure**, **complete**, **choose**. How must you change the base word for all but the first word?

3. (a) Which word is a compound? Make new words by changing the first part of the compound to **head**, then to **search**.

(b) Six words contain vowel pairs in which one letter is **i**. Write the six words. After each tell the sound the vowel pair makes.

4. Names in Words
Which words contain these names? Write the whole word. The spaces tell how many letters are needed.

D _ _ _ _ O N _ _ _   LE _ _ _ E

I _ A _ _ N _   _ _ _ D _ _ _ _ ES

_ _ _ P _ ETE   _ _ EVE _ _

5. Which Word Am I?
(a) I am what you do with a ruler.
(b) I am helpful in the dark.
(c) I am what you did for people who did not know each other.
(d) I am one thing you can do with your mind.
(e) I am a name given to three provinces.

6. What Did the Flashlight Show?
Write **flashlight** on your page as it is written below. Use the clues to find the words to write across **flashlight**. Then unscramble the circled letters to find out what the flashlight showed. All the words are in the list except the first one. It is in Unit 38.

Clues
a flat log boat
grassy area
National Hockey _____
not winning
pick
all done
where much wheat is grown
make up or pretend
short for **although**
model to follow

_ F _
L _ _ _
_ _ A _ _
_ _ S _ _ _
_ H _ _ _ _
_ _ _ _ L _ _ _
_ _ I _ _ _
_ _ _ G _ _
_ H _ _ _ _
_ _ T _ _ _

What did the flashlight show?

1. Which words
   (a) mean almost the same as **surely, finished, drill, encircle, model**?
   (b) could mean the opposite of **later, let loose, estimate, ugliness, reject**?
   (c) contain **quaint, vent, tern, media, lea**?

2. Roots
   Write two other words formed from each root below.
   (a) the root of **necessary** is **cess**
   (b) the root of **prevent** is **venire**, to come
   (c) the root of **introduced** is **ducere**, to lead
   (d) the root of **acquainted** is **cognoscere**, to know

3. Plus Four
   Write each word below. Beside each write four other words following the direction given.
   (a) **practice** plus four that end in **ice**
   (b) **surround** plus four that begin with **sur**
   (c) **measure** plus four that begin with **mea**
   (d) **pattern** plus four that end in **ern**

4. What's the Difference?
   Tell the difference in meaning between the words in the pairs below.
   (a) **introduced** and **acquainted**
   (b) **control** and **prevent**
   (c) **measure** and **pattern**
   (d) **certainly** and **necessary**

5. Lucky Seven

   Write **necessary** as it is written below. Use the clues to find the words that fit the spaces. Every word has seven letters. None are in this unit, but they are all in this book. When you have found all the words, do the second part of the puzzle.

   ```
   — — Ⓞ — — — —   N  hold in
   Ⓞ — — — — — —   E  a sample
   — — — Ⓞ — — —   C  what busy highways have
   — — Ⓞ — — — —   E  what you might do with a lemon
   Ⓞ — — — — — —   S  what you need for hot dogs
   — Ⓞ — — — — —   S  north-finder
   — — — — Ⓞ — —   A  oily province
   Ⓞ — — — — — —   R  Maritime delight
   Ⓞ — — — — — —   Y  thickly
   ```

   Now unscramble the circled letters to find the kind of year we hope you have had.

The 388 New Spelling Words in This Book

The number beside each word shows the page where the word is first listed in this book. The symbol (†) marks a word with a second spelling.

acquainted	26	camera	33	department	50
aerial	26	cement	76	dictionary	30
agree	78	certainly	81	difficulties	95
alarm	71	championship	6	direction	44
Alberta (Alta.)	60	cheap	74	dodge	9
allowed	78	cheat	93	double	15
aloud	58	cheek	93	downtown	42
alphabet	30	choose	30	drain	106
articles	18	chopped	106	drawer	95
ashes	26	chops	35		
assignment	30	chosen	56	eagle	15
association	44	cider	35	edge	97
attention	44	circle	15	education	44
attic	97	civic	56	elevator	60
audience	30	cloth	18	engagement	111
auditorium	33	clothed	18	enjoy	64
		clothing	18	equipment	28
backwards	81	code	109	equipped	30
baggage	109	compass	48	erect	91
basketball	46	complete	48	essay	33
beauty	33	contain	48	example	48
beef	35	continent	48	excellent	46
between	76	control	48	excitement	48
blame	71	convention	48	executive	48
blanket	18	cord	109	exercise	48
blaze	28	crust	12	exhibit	48
blizzard	28	cupboard	42	exhibition	48
board	6			extremely	81
bonfire	42	damp	74		
borrow	97	decoration	44	failed	78
broom	89	defeated	56	faithful	76
butterfly	42	defend	50	famous	74
button	18	delight	62	farther	81
		densely	81	†favour	58

film	64	index	33	machine	93
flakes	26	injure	95	machinery	93
flashlight	42	instruct	78	main	81
flour	12	instruction	44	major	6
force	71	instructor	46	mammal	15
fortune	97	instruments	95	Manitoba	
forward	81	introduced	111	(Man.)	60
fountain	58	invitation	44	manual	89
freedom	93	irrigation	106	measure	78
freeze	28	itch	26	members	56
frost	60	items	111	memory	30
fuel	89			mention	44
further	81	jacket	18	message	109
		jaw	95	metal	91
gasoline	60	jealous	76	missed	26
general	9	jelly	12	mist	64
gentle	15	join	78	mix	12
glare	109			modern	74
grain	60	keen	93	moose	89
gravel	60	kettle	15	mosquitoes	28
gravy	35	key	93	mower	106
greet	78	kindly	81	museum	33
grip	71	kitchen	12		
guard	46	knees	95	napkins	35
		knot	71	nation	56
handlebars	42	knowledge	9	necessary	60
haul	60			†neighbour	58
hawk	76	†labour	58	New Brunswick	
heaven	91	ladder	106	(N.B.)	64
hollow	74	lawn	111	news	91
holy	74	league	6	Nova Scotia	
hose	106	lemonade	35	(N.S.)	64
huge	89	length	18	nowhere	81
husband	111	liberty	33	numerous	58
hymn	111	limb	95		
		liner	64	oar	26
iceberg	42	loan	97	oatmeal	42
idle	15	lobster	64	object	44
imagine	9	lose	6	objectives	30
immediately	50	losing	6	offered	50
important	56			onion	35

opposite	50	prove	89	scarce	109
orchard	106	provide	50	scissors	18
organization	28	province	56	screen	93
Ottawa	56	pudding	35	search	71
outboard	42	pure	74	section	44
oven	12	puzzle	28	service	56
overalls	42			settle	15
		racket	6	settlement	15
paragraph	30	radar	109	shelter	97
parka	26	raft	109	shock	71
parliament	56	rainbow	109	shoulder	58
patch	71	raisin	26	shower	106
pattern	18	rapid	74	signal	6
paved	60	receipt	97	silly	74
pepper	35	recipe	12	simple	15
per cent	33	record	64	skirt	18
personal	15	refrigerator	9	slice	12
petroleum	33	region	56	smoke	109
photograph	42	regular	50	smooth	89
pickles	35	rent	97	soccer	46
pier	64	repair	60	soup	12
pitcher	6	restaurant	33	sour	12
polish	95	returned	50	spade	106
polite	74	review	30	speedometer	42
pollution	44	rink	46	spider	26
popsicle	15	rise	26	spill	78
position	44	risk	6	spoil	64
poured	58	rodeo	76	spoon	12
practice	6	roses	33	sprinkle	106
practises	6	rotten	97	spruce	106
prairie	60	rough	62	square	28
prepare	44	royal	15	squeeze	28
press	111	rural	56	steal	6
prevent	44			steering	93
Prince Edward		saddle	76	sting	71
Island (P.E.I.)	64	salad	35	stir	12
prison	33	sandwiches	35	stole	6
projector	30	Saskatchewan		stool	26
promote	50	(Sask.)	60	strap	71
proof	89	satisfied	78	strikes	6
properly	81	saucer	12	studied	78
property	97	sausage	9	study	93

studying	30	topic	30	waves	71
subway	50	torn	78	weak	74
surround	58	tough	62	weave	18
surrounded	58	towel	18	wedding	111
sweep	93	traffic	60	weigh	62
swept	26	transcontin-		whip	71
swift	74	ental	60	whistle	71
switch	76	treat	93	who's	89
		trial	15	whose	89
tame	74	truth	89	wieners	33
taxi	93	turtle	15	wife	111
tennis	46	typewriter	42	wives	111
terrible	74			†woollen	18
terrific	74	union	89	worth	97
terror	109	unite	111	wound	58
theatre	33	urban	56	wrapped	111
thirsty	35			wrist	95
though	58	view	64		
thumb	95	vinegar	35	yeast	12
ticket	26	visitor	64		
timber	97	volleyball	42	zero	28
toast	12	voyage	9		

Second Spellings

If your teacher allows it, you may use these spellings of the words listed below. Also listed is the number of the page on which each word first appears.

favor	58
labor	58
neighbor	58
woolen	18

The 49 Extra Words for Good Spellers

Good spellers will learn many more than 49 extra words from the spelling exercises and other work, but these are included, in separate colour blocks, on the pages shown.

absorb	50	daisy	106	motto	46
alley	93	defence	50		
average	97	deny	78	offence	76
axle	15	drown	26		
				plough	62
biscuit	35	elementary	30		
bleeding	95			scheme	109
blessing	111	failure	56	secure	89
bough	62			stitch	18
branch	106	grease	93	stumble	15
bruise	95			synagogue	9
		hesitate	44	syrup	12
calves	26	hinge	9		
celery	35			tanned	74
clever	74	jewellery	111	target	109
colonies	56			texts	30
colony	56	keel	93		
contour	48			utensil	89
copy	78	lacrosse	46		
correspond	48	ledge	9	vanished	78
cradle	15	lodge	97		
curtains	18			yolk	26

282 Most Commonly Misspelled Words

Of all the words listed so far in The Macmillan Spelling Series, these are the ones which many pupils have the most trouble spelling correctly. You should know them all by now.

about	brother	disappear
acquainted	brought	disappointed
across	built	divide
address	business	doctor
afternoon	busy	does
again	buy	done
all right		don't
almost	cannot	down
along	can't	dropped
already	captain	
always	certainly	early
am	children	Easter
among	choose	easy
amount	chosen	eighth
answer	Christmas	enough
any	close	equipped
April	clothes	every
are	colour	everybody
asked	come	excellent
aunt	complete	excuse
	control	
balloon	cough	father
basketball	could	February
beauty	country	finally
because	course	fine
been	cousin	first
before		for
begin	day	forty
beginning	dear	fourth
believe	decided	Friday
bought	didn't	friend
boy	different	from
break	dining	fun

getting
goes
good
good-bye
grade
guess
guest

had
half
handkerchiefs
happiness
has
have
hear
heard
hello
her
here
him
his
hope
hospital
hour
house
how

I'm
immediately
in
instead
interesting
isn't
it
it's
its

just

knew
know
knowledge

laid
lead
league
led
lessons
letter
library
like
little
loose
lose
losing
lots

make
many
maybe
meant
minute
Miss
morning
mother
Mr.
Mrs.
much
my

name
necessary
neighbour
never
ninety
ninth
none
now

o'clock
October
off
often
on
once

one
our
out
outside

paid
passed
people
perhaps
piece
play
pleasant
please
practice
pretty
prevent
principal
probably

question
quiet
quit
quite

raise
ready
real
receive
remember
right

said
sandwiches
Saturday
saw
says
school
scissors
seemed
send
separate
several

shoes
shoulder
since
sincerely
soldier
some
soon
speech
store
straight
studying
sugar
summer
Sunday
suppose
sure
surprise

teacher
tear
the
their
them
then
there
they

think
though
thought
threw
through
time
to
today
together
tomorrow
too
toward
toys
train
tries
trouble
Tuesday
twelfth
two

uncle
until
us
usually

very

was
wear
weather
Wednesday
week
well
were
when
where
whether
which
while
white
whole
whose
wieners
with
woman
won't
would
write
written
wrote

your

Tables of Useful Words

Provinces and Major Cities

British Columbia (B.C.)	Victoria, Vancouver
Alberta (Alta.)	Edmonton, Calgary
Saskatchewan (Sask.)	Regina, Saskatoon
Manitoba (Man.)	Winnipeg
Ontario (Ont.)	Toronto, Ottawa
Quebec (Que.)	Quebec, Montreal
New Brunswick (N.B.)	Fredericton, Saint John
Nova Scotia (N.S.)	Halifax
Prince Edward Island (P.E.I.)	Charlottetown
Newfoundland (Nfld.)	St. John's

Measurement

Celsius	C	kilometre	km
centimetre	cm	litre	L
gram	g	metre	m
hectare	ha	millilitre	mL
kilogram	kg	millimetre	mm

87 97 08 18 28 38 48 58 68 BP 9 8 7 6 5 4 3 2 1